Presented To:

_____

From:

_____

Date:

_____

WHERE'S
MY
EDWARD?

BOOKS BY LAURA B. GALLIER

Choosing to Wait

Why Wait?

AVAILABLE FROM DESTINY IMAGE PUBLISHERS

WHERE'S MY EDWARD?

Seeking a
FOREVER Romance

LAURA GALLIER

DESTINY IMAGE® PUBLISHERS, INC.

P.O. Box 310, Shippensburg, PA 17257-0310

"Speaking to the Purposes of God for This Generation and for the Generations to Come."

This book and all other Destiny Image, Revival Press, MercyPlace, Fresh Bread, Destiny Image Fiction, and Treasure House books are available at Christian bookstores and distributors worldwide.

For a U.S. bookstore nearest you, call 1-800-722-6774.

For more information on foreign distributors, call 717-532-3040.

Reach us on the Internet: www.destinyimage.com.

ISBN 13 TP: 978-0-7684-3806-2

ISBN 13 HC: 978-0-7684-3807-9

ISBN 13 LP: 978-0-7684-3808-6

ISBN 13 Ebook: 978-0-7684-8987-3

For Worldwide Distribution, Printed in the U.S.A.

1 2 3 4 5 6 7 8 9 10 11 / 13 12 11

To my husband Patrick,

The storm of shattered hopes blew in.
At the time, I could not see
How brightly the sun would shine the day
The Lord introduced you to me.

LAURA

Where is My Edward? This book is a must read for all women, single and married. When I read the title, I couldn't wait to read the book. I started and couldn't stop—it was like a delicious piece of cake that you want to gobble down yet pausing to savor every bite. I enthusiastically recommend that every female give herself the gift of this wonderful book.

JACKIE KENDALL
Best-selling author of *Lady in Waiting*

All I can say is 'WOW!' I could not put the book down. It is the best material I have ever read on the topic of love and romance. I cannot wait until it is published. I want to buy copies for all of my female relatives and friends.

SONIA, 42 years old

As a Christian bookstore manager and single woman in my thirties, I've read nearly every relationship book that has gone to print in the last ten years. That said, this one tops the charts. You brought such balance to the issue of romance by giving women hope that true love is still alive, while at the same time exposing the lies and deceptions that Hollywood impresses on young girls and women today. Your book speaks to the deeper issues in a woman's heart, and it gripped me from the very first page to the last.

RACHAEL, 33 years old

OK, let's just say every college girl needs to read this! The good news is that with the *Twilight* theme, I know my friends will want to. It's great that you found something that interests young people in order to get them interested enough to buy the book. I read it with the goal of making comments about what to fix, but I didn't find a thing! It is just so good.

RACHEL, 20 years old

Contents

TORN

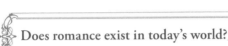

Does romance exist in today's world?

"The way he watches you—it's so...protective. Like he's about to throw himself in front of a bullet to save you or something."

I laughed, though I was still not able to meet her gaze. "That's a bad thing?"

"No." She frowned as she struggled for the words. "It's just different. He's very intense about you...and very careful. I feel like I don't understand your relationship. Like there's something secret I'm missing..."

"I think you're imagining things, Mom,"...

"The way you move—you orient yourself around him without even thinking about it. When he moves, even a little bit, you adjust your position at the same time. Like magnets...or gravity. You're like a...satellite, or something. I've never seen anything like it."

*B*ella Swan. The mere mention of her name carries undeniable implications of love and romance. I can't say that I've seen a swan lately, but I do know that they are majestic birds, the embodiment of beauty and grace. Unlike the majority of nature's creatures, swans are loyal to *one* mate for life and remain side by side as inseparable lovebirds year round. Combine this rich imagery with the first name *Bella,* meaning "beautiful," and it appears *Twilight's* leading lady was clearly destined to fall deeply in love for a lifetime with an equally love-struck man.

What about you? Do you believe lasting love is in your future? Do you consider yourself a beautiful swan, or do you feel more like an ugly duckling? Are your hopes of romance at an all-time high, or are you currently discouraged and disappointed? Having personally been through the desolate valleys of loneliness and broken relationships, and also rising to the breathtaking mountaintops that accompany a lasting love connection, I can identify with you either way.

Whether you are single, dating, engaged, or married, it is my prayer and belief that the Lord will use this book to speak to you about your romantic hopes and desires. After all, the *Twilight* characters and plot originated in Stephenie Meyer's imagination, but *God* is writing *your* personal love story. Furthermore, His plans for you are more than fiction; God intends that His will become a reality in your life. If such knowledge is new to you, keep reading. I will continue to expound on how your love life is near and dear to the heart of God.

Using the *Twilight* series as our reference point and the Bible as our standard of truth, each chapter of this book is designed to offer solid advice and sound answers to your most pressing love-related uncertainties and questions. In the process of separating fact from fiction, we will discover numerous truths about men and women, relationships, and lasting love commitments, all for the purpose of pointing you in the direction of your own *Twilight*-kind of romance.

FALLING FOR EDWARD

I think you'll agree with me that from the instant Bella crosses paths with her "wealthy guardian"—the English translation for *Edward*—she is inexplicably drawn to him in a way that defies logic and supersedes cautious rules of romance. She doesn't *learn* to love Edward or *grow* to love him in time; she *falls* desperately in love with him in such a powerful and intense way that it seems beyond her ability to resist or reason with her feelings. And why would she? Edward is the fulfillment of her heart's every desire, her modern-day prince in supernatural armor.

Then we have Bella's mom, Renee. Wouldn't you say that she adheres to more of a "head-over-heart" approach to love and commitment? Perhaps she has never had the privilege of experiencing the heart-pounding, gut-wrenching, earth-shaking emotions that rock a woman's world upon finding and falling for that one-and-only soul mate. Then again, maybe Renee has been wounded, her dreams of romance shattered by the reality of faded love and a failed marriage. One thing is certain; Renee has reasons for approaching love with caution and for continually advising Bella to do the same.

Where do you stand? Are you willing and ready to take a swan dive into love and romance, or do you prefer to stick your neatly manicured toe into the unpredictable tides of commitment and proceed with guarded caution? More to the point, do you believe that romance and lasting love actually exist in today's world?

A WOUNDED GENERATION

It's estimated that over 50 percent of American couples today choose to cohabitate, either before marriage or in lieu of a marital commitment altogether. Furthermore, approximately *one* out of every *four* American single women (ages 25 to 39) currently lives with her boyfriend.[2]

While many modern-day movies and television shows portray cohabitation as a trendy final step in the "dating game," I can assure you, there's more than *trendiness* at work here. The truth is we live in a wounded generation. On the one hand, multitudes of singles are afraid of "till death do us part" commitments—and it's no wonder! The prevalence of infidelity, marital discord, and divorce are enough to breed skepticism in any rational person. To add to our apprehension, it seems mainstream society now applauds promiscuity and mocks long-term monogamy as an unrealistic and unsatisfying lifestyle.

On the other hand, there's *Twilight*. Stephenie Meyer's book series has currently sold over *85 million* copies worldwide. You know what that means? This generation has *not* lost the desire for romance and lasting love! We are captivated by Edward and Bella's love affair because, if the truth be told, we, too, long to be connected with "the one"—that handsome soul mate with whom we share such intense mutual chemistry and a heartfelt connection that we cling to one another, faithfully, for life. We'll take a closer look at what draws us to the *Twilight* saga in an upcoming chapter. For now, it's important to note that it is *not* a desire for lasting love that's missing in this generation. What many of us truly lack is the *wisdom* to find and sustain a healthy love relationship and the *courage* to embrace commitment. It is for this reason—to bring encouragement and enlightenment in the area of love and romance—that I pour my heart out to you in this book.

I believe in lasting love. I also believe we must learn how to cultivate it. As we seek to experience our own *Twilight*-kind of romance, we need a balance of both—Bella's willingness to become vulnerable for the sake of love and Renee's dependence on principles that help us overcome relationship traps and pitfalls.

Speaking of traps, we need to do some soul searching and determine if our own insecurities, self doubt, and feelings of unworthiness are holding us back from making a love connection in the first place.

YOU'RE WORTH IT

Do you believe that you are worthy of love, adoration, and a man's faithful commitment?

Since we tend to attract what we think we deserve, your plight to find lasting love begins with how you feel about that person who stares back at you in the mirror everyday. Unless you feel worthy of being in a relationship with a handsome, godly man who treats you with the utmost respect, you never will be.

Keep in mind, your worth is not measured by the things people have said about you or done to you throughout your life. Your value comes from *God*. How valuable are you to Him? There is no measurement that could possibly define it, but there is a cross that displays it. *You are worth dying for.*

What liberty we find when we trade *self*-esteem for *God*-esteem, relying on what God's Word says about us rather than looking solely to our own abilities or circumstances for validation. Once you settle that you are worthy of a man's love and adoration, you have taken the first step toward finding and sustaining a relationship with "Edward"—your mate for life.

Whether you are struggling through challenges with your spouse or wrestling with anxiety about finding the right guy, one thing is certain—*he is worth it!*

HE'S WORTH IT

I saw a bumper sticker the other day that said, "God made man before woman, proof that even God has rough drafts." As we'll explore in an upcoming chapter, we live in a fallen world where animosity spreads like a disease, infecting and provoking men and women in a never-ending vicious gender war. Men complain about women and their insatiable needs and demands while women grumble about men and their inability to live up to their expectations. In the end, both men and women are dissatisfied and blame their frustration on the opposite sex.

As you progress through this book, however, you will discover that our gender-specific differences are actually by God's design. Furthermore, when understood and embraced, these differences can become the very catalyst that fuels unity and companionship within a love relationship.

Achieving lasting love may look easy on the big screen, but in real life, it takes a considerable amount of work. Married ladies, your husband is worth the effort. (I realize some days, it might not seem so.) To my single friends, your future spouse is worthy of all the sacrifice and determination required of you in order to lay a strong foundation for what lies ahead.

Men are at the center of *romance*, both figuratively and literally (ro-*man*-ce). If we're going to experience a love connection on caliber with our *Twilight* sweeties, Edward and Bella, we have to realize that our "Edward" is worth it! He deserves our loyalty, respect, and admiration. (We'll look at how that actually applies in everyday life a little later.)

LASTING LOVE IS WORTH IT

How would you have felt if, upon reading the final chapters of *Breaking Dawn*, Edward and Bella suddenly became plagued by a host of marital incompatibilities, and the last few pages of the four-book series described their painful divorce? That would have been horrible, right? I'm fairly confident I would have hurled my book, shredded and burned, clear across the room!

As real as Edward and Bella may seem in our hearts, we know they are just fictional characters. If it hurts us to think about *their* relationship coming to a tragic end, think about *real* couples calling it quits. There are half-empty family photo albums all across America— captions of family outings, celebrations, and cherished moments come to an unsettling halt as Mom and Dad announce they are divorcing.

A fellow student and friend in my daughter's sixth-grade science class was recently shedding tears uncontrollably. As you well know, sixth-grade boys avoid crying in front of their peers at all costs, so my daughter knew something was seriously wrong. As it turns out, the 12-year-old boy learned the night before that his mom and dad were divorcing. To add to his shock and confusion, his mother announced that she already had a boyfriend. The proverbial rug was ripped out from under that young man, and he struggled to comprehend life now that his foundation, his family, would never stand as a united household again.

Why am I telling you this? I'm not trying to depress you, and I am certainly not attempting to heap guilt on you if you've been through a divorce. What I *am* trying to convey is that, while love and romance do entail goose bumps, fun date nights, and spontaneous laughter, there is a *much* bigger picture we must keep in mind. In the long run, the rise or fall of a family is dependent on a man and a woman's love and commitment toward one another. That said, when we talk about your romantic hopes and dreams of loving for a lifetime, we are ultimately talking about family, even if as of now you are too young to get married and would settle for simply finding a somewhat attractive guy to take you to the next school dance.

Suffice it to say, lasting love is worth it. It's worth starting and finishing this book, worth renewing our minds to healthier ways of relating to the opposite sex, and worth all of the associated risks and rewards. Creating a legacy of love that will benefit our children, grandchildren, and generations to come—now that's worth it! (And the goose bumps have their merit, too.)

TWILIGHT MANIA

Are you a fan of the *Twilight* series, or did you cross over into all-out obsession? Perhaps you are one of the rebels who never really bought into the *Twilight* hysteria. No matter the case, as we venture further into our pursuit of truth concerning our desire for a *Twilight*-kind of romance, there are profound realities to be discovered as we come to understand *why* women are so drawn to the *Twilight* story in the first place. That's the subject of our first chapter, but before turning there, I encourage you to take time and prayerfully consider the questions posed in the *Reflections on Romance* questions below. You might be surprised by the number of significant insights you've gained after reading just the introduction.

You know you're obsessed with *Twilight* if at any time:

- You bought a pillowcase with either Edward or Jacob's face on it.
- You exchanged your self-tanning cream for stark white body powder.
- You actually clicked on one of those online links that promises you an audition for a part in the next *Twilight* movie.
- You own a *Twilight* shower curtain.
- You've spent time arguing with people about why they should be on "Team Edward" or "Team Jacob."
- When you see a silver C30 Volvo, you speed up to see who is driving.
- You've promised yourself that before you die, you will take a trip to Forks, Washington—or move there.
- You no longer fear running with wolves.

REFLECTIONS ON
ROMANCE—INTRODUCTION

1. How important is romantic love to you, and why?

   _____

   _____

   _____

   _____

2. Who do you identify with most: Bella's tendency to plunge into love or Renee's more cautious approach to romance? Why do you think you're this way?

   _____

   _____

   _____

   _____

3. In your opinion, what might be some consequences of failing to see the unrealistic, fantasy-based elements in the *Twilight* love story?

   _____

   _____

_____

_____

4. Do you see yourself as worthy of a man's lifetime commitment and love? Journal your thoughts on this topic.

_____

_____

_____

_____

5. Do you struggle with feelings of animosity toward men? If so, think about why that may be and journal your conclusions.

_____

_____

_____

_____

PRAYER

Lord, I thank You that You know and love me. I am comforted that You care about my desire for romance, and I commit my love life into Your competent hands. Please help me to be led by Your Spirit as I seek romance. As I commit to learn more about Your plan for love and intimacy, reveal truth to me. Answer my heart's questions, and expose any areas of false belief that I may unknowingly be esteeming as truth. Be with me every minute of every day, and help me to sense Your love for me. In Jesus' name, amen.

Endnotes

1. Stephenie Meyer, *Eclipse* (New York: Hachette Book Group, 2007), 67-68.
2. Christina Gregorie, "Cohabitation and Marriage In America—Study: The State of Our Unions 2009—Living Together vs. Getting Married," January 25, 2010, http://divorce.suite101.com/article.cfm/cohabitation_and_marriage_in_america_2009.

Chapter One

CAPTIVATED

What draws us to the Twilight love story?

My husband and I went to see New Moon
*the weekend it was released. Having navi-
gated our way through a rambunctious, loud-
mouthed crowd and successfully gotten hold of
two coveted tickets, we thought the most stressful
part of our evening was over. We were wrong.
After handing our tickets to the guy in the black
vest and red bowtie, we were sent to the back
of a line that stretched all the way outside and
wrapped nearly halfway around the building!
All of this just to enter our theater.*

Quickly acquainting ourselves with the people
next to us in line, we joined forces and began
a militant operation of exposing line cutters. Anyone
who tried to cheat the system and blend in ahead of
us suffered extreme humiliation as our group pointed

them out and tattled on them. Yes, it was a bit juvenile, but somehow we derived great satisfaction watching cheaters get escorted to the very back of the line. Besides, it was a great way to pass the time as we waited on the line to move—while shivering in the cold, I might add.

I felt like I was running with the bulls in Pamplona when the theater doors finally opened and we were given a green light by "Mr. Bowtie" to enter. I have a feeling herds of cattle are probably more polite to one another than some of the people were as they galloped and kicked to find seats. By the time Patrick and I settled into our chairs, it seemed like we had mastered a triathlon. Like a cut-throat game of musical chairs, *Twilight* fans resorted to all-out sprinting in order to fill the last few available seats. One panicked lady in particular leapt over an entire row of people and, to my amazement, landed in an empty chair. (I hoped that there was no popcorn tub in that seat.)

WHAT'S ALL THE FUSS ABOUT?

What is it about the *Twilight* storyline that has captivated millions of people, especially women? Furthermore, how is it that the books and movies appeal to females from such a wide array of ages and stages of life? I've seen sixth-grade girls with a mouthful of braces reading one of the *Twilight* books, grinning about something in the text. I've witnessed high school girls and college graduates sporting "Team Edward" and "Team Jacob" T-shirts. I have also attended a parent assembly at my kids' middle school where I overheard moms talking about their love for the *Twilight* saga.

Surely there is more to this phenomenon than Jacob's abs or Edward's superpowers. Aren't there lots of books and movie plots featuring muscular men and heroes with uncommon abilities?

Believe it or not, I think the answer to the *Twilight* hysteria is deeply rooted in the female heart. Allow me to explain. As I just mentioned, I saw the movie *New Moon.* If you saw the movie, too, you likely remember the final scene, but more than that, you probably recall how Edward's words made you *feel.* After a brief confrontation between Bella, Jacob, and Edward, Bella pleads to be transformed into a vampire, to which Edward replies, "Under one condition." Sitting in the theater, a deafening silence filled the auditorium as pounding hearts anticipated his explanation.

"Marry me."

And with those two simple words, my stomach did a flip-flop, and my heart leapt! I've been on some serious mega coasters in my life, but I must say, none of them came close to producing the emotional high

I experienced sitting motionless in my theater chair that night. My heart responded with such intensity to Edward's request that, to my surprise, my eyes dampened. I know I was not alone in my reaction because, in that moment, the theater audience let out an adoring, unified sigh.

How did Patrick respond to that scene? He jumped out of his seat—not because he was so moved by the dialog, but because he was hoping I too would hop up quickly and we could beat the large crowd out of the parking lot. Translation: His reaction was *nothing* like mine.

I've said it before, and I'll say it again—*men and women are different, very different!* Things that appeal to men do not necessarily get our attention, and conversely, experiences that move us to the core of our being may seem boring and irrelevant to men. That doesn't make one gender right and the other gender wrong; it simply makes us different.

More about guy-girl differences later. Back to the last scene in *New Moon*.

Why did it grab me so much? *Because I long to be adored by a man.* Notice I didn't say I long to be "liked" or "accepted," much less "used" by a man. No, I want to be *deeply treasured.* As a result, the way Edward pursues and cherishes Bella causes "bells and whistles" to go off in my soul. Just like the sight of a steak makes a hungry man salivate, my romantic thirst is stirred in the presence of a passionate, loyal, love-obsessed man. Even though I am married and my husband *does* treasure me, I still find the intensity and chemistry between Bella and Edward incredibly enticing.

WHAT ABOUT YOU?

I bet you, too, long to know that a man is *captivated* by you, that he is totally blown away by your beauty, personality, and uniqueness. Some of us desire this more than others, but as a general rule, females tend to possess an internal craving to be fervently sought after by a man we love and respect.

In addition, most of us can identify with a strong, inner longing to experience authentic romantic intimacy with a man. As we'll see in the next chapter, this tendency in females is by God's design. For now, let's agree that Stephenie Meyer managed to write a story that pulls our souls' deeply rooted desires to the very surface of our awareness. Like an arrow that pierces through the core of an apple, *Twilight* penetrates our hearts because, deep down, we want what Bella has—adventure, passion, intimacy, and a perfect man who seems to exist to love and protect her. And as if *one* heroic guy isn't enough, Bella also has Jacob in hot pursuit, another dreamy guy who would die for her without thinking twice about it.

Some of us are more moved by the story than others, but at the end of the day, if you're reading this book, it's likely because the *Twilight* series touched you in a significant way.

What's so important about understanding why we're moved by the "Twilight" story? Allow me to answer by sharing an analogy. Do you ever get the munchies? I sure do! (I'm feeling them coming on right now, to tell you the truth!) When I'm plagued by the munchies, I open my refrigerator, take a look around, then head over to the pantry and scan the shelves for something appealing. Next, I open the cabinet where my husband and I stash goodies, and I take inventory of what I have to choose from. Eventually I snack on something, but a few minutes later, I find myself making the rounds in our kitchen again—refrigerator, pantry, goodie stash.

The problem with the munchies is that we're experiencing a craving sensation, but we can't seem to actually identify what it is that we're craving! As a result, we walk around aimlessly, most often eating things that aren't good for us. Then, with our appetite still nagging, we feel just as dissatisfied as we leave the kitchen as we did when we first entered.

And so it can be with our desires for romance and intimacy…

MUNCHIES OF THE SOUL

If we don't know what is it that's motivating us—what that deep internal sense of longing is that's resonating in our souls—we'll go through life looking for something to satisfy us, only to discover that we never quite find it. We'll look for love and acceptance in the wrong places, perhaps entering into relationships with guys that we have no business dating, and we'll find that no matter how hard we try, the emotional "munchies" never go away.

Once we know and understand what it is that our souls are longing for, however, we can stop making rounds in the proverbial kitchen of life and begin making more deliberate, productive choices. For example, if it's an authentic, meaningful intimate connection we're looking for with a man, we know that we have no business dating some guy who is just looking to have his way with us sexually. On the other hand, if we *don't* understand the thirst in our soul, we may actually give casual sex or promiscuity a try, thinking connecting with men *physically* will somehow subdue our *emotional* cravings. It won't, of course. It will actually leave us more dissatisfied and destitute at heart than ever.

As another example, once we realize that what we *really* want is to be treasured by a man, there's no point in dating a guy who mistreats us and insults us. Am I right? OK, one last example. It's been said that the root of all substance addiction is a need to feel loved. If an alcoholic or drug abuser doesn't know that, however, he or she will keep attempting to fill that void with chemicals that can never possibly provide what is truly needed.

So in summary, it's important to know why you are drawn to the *Twilight* series because it is most likely the result of your soul's romantic wishes—pure, innocent, genuine desires. Furthermore, once we *identify* and *understand* those desires, we can then avoid counterfeit methods of satisfying them.

THE FATHER FACTOR

What do you think of Charlie, Bella's dad? He seems wonderful to me, but that could be because I grew up with very little contact with my father and always admired girls who had caring dads in their lives. My parents separated when my mom was pregnant with me. I grew up with my big sister (who is now my best friend), but since I had no brother and my mom never remarried, I was far removed from any significant male presence.

As a child and teenager, I never had that sense that a man, my father, was looking out for me. I didn't realize at the time how much not having a fatherly presence in my life affected me, but I want to discuss it with you in case you too have been impacted by *the father factor*.

As previously stated, we tend to long for a man to find us captivating, and we also seek to experience a meaningful, intimate connection with a man. As little girls, those emotional needs are present, but they have yet to mature into romantic desires. With this in mind, it is God's ingenious plan that a father's love and attention fill the longing in his daughter's young heart. However, when we have an absentee or uninterested father, or we are abused by him or another father figure, it is an assault on our delicate, impressionable souls. Girls who suffer this internal wound usually respond in one of two ways during the teen years and perhaps even throughout adulthood if their wound remains unhealed.

THE DESPERATE RESPONSE

One response is that of total desperation and infatuation with receiving attention from guys. We are starved for male affirmation so we seek it in pretty much any form we can find it. We look to romantic relationships to compensate for the lack of acceptance, affection, and validation we aren't receiving, or never did receive, at home.

I recently spoke with girls who, as sophomores and juniors in high school, had already given birth to babies. The two things they seemed to have in common were an absent or uninterested father and a much older boyfriend. The attention these girls received from their twenty-something-year-old seductive baby-daddies is a counterfeit for what they lack from their fathers. Not realizing this, they become entangled in complicated relationships with guys who do not have their best interest at heart.

> "The absence of a father, especially in a young person's life, is a strong factor associated with adolescent sexual activity."[2]

Sometimes I sit back and watch the way my husband interacts with my daughters. He hugs them, affirms how beautiful and precious they are, and welcomes them to snuggle next to him on the sofa and watch movies. It's something I never had growing up. If that's your story, too, know that you likely have a heightened, perhaps even seriously out of balance, desire for male attention. That is, unless the Lord has healed you of that wound or you find yourself responding in the opposite way...

THE INDIFFERENT RESPONSE

Having been hurt by an absentee, neglectful, or abusive father, some young girls grow to despise men. It's not something they necessarily say out loud to themselves, but nonetheless, it is something they harbor in the depths of their hearts and continually act upon. They are afraid to trust men. For them, a desire for romance is a weakness, a horrible vulnerability that's to be suppressed and resisted. Even if they enter into marriage, they will hold back emotionally, fearing being too open and trusting will backfire on them. A woman like this will be cynical toward the man in her life, and even though her sarcasm and insults are obviously hurtful to him, she would rather "punch him" before he "punches her."

Perhaps that's you, but then, what are you doing reading a book about romance? Maybe you are seeking freedom from indifference toward men, and it took courage just to pick up and start this book. If that's the case, you go girl! As a matter of fact, *all* of us need to go...*to God*.

GO TO GOD

Are you sailing smoothly on the sea of love right now or going through a challenging time? Perhaps you are single and feeling a bit lonely, or married and wondering where the passion has gone. If you are suffering in the romance department, don't drown yourself in Blue Bell or attempt to shop your way into contentment. Prayerfully identify and admit what it is that your soul is crying out for, then take that need to the One who created your very soul.

Do you remember that part in *New Moon* where Edward has rejected Bella and disappeared from her life, and Bella drops to her knees and prays for God to comfort her wounded heart? That's OK, neither do I, because Bella did not respond that way. When Edward leaves her for a time, Bella doesn't turn to God with her soul's needs; she turns within, which is why she spirals into a dark depression and can't seem to find any sense of hope or joy.

Does God care when we feel lonely, impatient for love, or fearful that our marriage has lost its spark once and for all? Of course He does! This is God we're talking about. He's the one who took the time to put adorable tiny black dots on the back of ladybugs and made butterfly wings more exquisite than the finest of man-made fabrics. *God cares about the details, and that includes the details of your life!* That's why First Peter 5:7 says, *"Cast all your anxiety on …*[God] *because He cares for you."*

To be anxious is to be overwhelmed. What are you overwhelmed about? What situations in your life are making you feel helpless and afraid? Don't just *tell* God about it; do what the Scripture says; *cast your anxiety on God.* Just like a child who's unable to tie her shoes is quick to prop her feet up on Daddy's lap so he can tie the laces, lay that problem or need in God's lap. It doesn't mean He'll instantly fix it, but you can rest assured that He *will* intervene in *His* timing and *His* way.

Now don't go taking matters into your own hands while you're waiting on God's intervention and solution. And don't be surprised when, while you're fixated on getting an answer to prayer, God is more focused on transforming your *character.*

Perhaps you've never thought of Him this way, but God is the *ultimate* relationship expert. He's better at orchestrating love matches than eHarmony and can give you more wisdom during a moment spent in prayer than Dr. Phil can give you in a lifetime of counseling sessions. How silly we are to ignore God, rebel against His biblical instructions, and try to fix everything ourselves while the God of all creation is beckoning us to *"...approach the throne of grace with confidence, so that we may receive mercy and find grace to help us in our time of need"* (Heb. 4:16).

I'll say it again—we need to go to God!

In the next chapter, we'll answer the question, *"What ignites and sustains attraction?"* But first, consider the following *Reflections on Romance* questions, and take note of your thoughts. Then snuggle up with the Lord in prayer and allow Him to speak to your heart as only He can.

REFLECTIONS ON ROMANCE—CHAPTER 1

1. Do you long to be adored by a man and desire a meaningful, intimate romantic relationship? Write about these desires and how they are currently affecting you.

_____

_____

_____

_____

2. Do you have "munchies" of the soul? In what ways are you trying to satisfy internal longings, only to find you come up short?

_____

_____

_____

_____

3. Think about your relationship with your father. Did he affirm your value and worth or somehow disappoint you? How has this perhaps affected the way you view men and romantic relationships?

_____

_____

_____

_____

4. What are you overwhelmed or worried about? Are you willing to trust God to intervene in your life and provide the direction and help you need?

_____

_____

_____

_____

5. What attracts you to a guy?

_____

_____

_____

_____

PRAYER

Lord, there is nothing shameful about a woman's desire to be pursued and loved by a man. Please help me to understand these desires in my own heart and manage them *in a way that honors You. Forgive me for the times I have ignored You and painstakingly tried to solve issues in my life that I needed to simply entrust to You. Help me to realize how much You love me and care about the details of my life, including my dreams of love and romance. Heal me from wounds of the past, and prepare me for the future plans You have in store for me. Help me to look to You as the ultimate Father. In Jesus' name I pray, amen.*

Endnotes

1. Stephenie Meyer, *New Moon* (New York: Hachette Book Group USA, 2006), 563.
2. Diane E. Papalia, Sally Wendokos Olds, Ruth Duskin Feldman, *A Child's Developing World, Infancy Through Adolescence,* 11th ed. (New York: McGraw-Hill Higher Education, 2008).

Chapter Two

INTRIGUED

 What ignites and sustains attraction?

*One thing is certain; Edward and Bella clearly experienced an intense mutual attraction the minute their paths crossed. Sure, the idea that Bella gave off some irresistible scent while standing across the room from Edward is a bit...well...odd. But what is it in **real** life that causes two unfamiliar souls to make eye contact and simultaneously feel intense shared chemistry?*

There is no actual scientific explanation for attraction, but studies do show that, while outer appearances may initially get our attention, our interest will quickly dwindle if we pick up on irritating personality traits. We are usually drawn to those with whom we have a lot in common, yet our feelings of attraction tend to soar when we meet someone who possesses qualities we *wish* we had. This explains why the introverted "Bellas" of the world are often drawn to bad-boy "Edwards." Girls who *wish* they had the courage to take more risks and live life on the edge will feel inexplicably fascinated by guys who do.

Edward and Bella aren't the first pair to experience love at first sight. Believe it or not, the earth's very first couple fell head over heels when they met.

THE ORIGINAL LOVE STORY

Perhaps you've heard the Genesis account of creation and wondered if it's some farfetched fairy tale. I wish I had time to expound on the reliability and accuracy of the Bible, but in an effort to stay on topic, allow me to simply ask, where do you believe love comes from? What causes a man to die for a woman or a woman to forsake all others for one man? Is love the result of a random evolutionary process or something far more profound and spiritual? We know it cannot be examined under a microscope; does this mean love is not real?

While there is no litmus test that empirically proves the Bible is the inspired Word of God, there is plenty of evidence that indicates it is a supernatural book. And just as love is best proven by those who dare to act on it, so the Bible's truths become an inescapable reality by those who passionately live by them.

Now on to the story of the earth's very first lovers.

Adam was created by God out of dirt. Is that why little boys are so drawn to mud? Anyway, Adam was here before Eve and was clearly designed by God to find great fulfillment in productivity. He named all of God's creatures and tended to his surroundings—a garden paradise. It was *God* who decided that Adam needed a soul mate, so He put Adam in a deep sleep and removed one of his ribs. Then, with care and preciseness, God used Adam's rib to sculpt a new masterpiece—Eve.

Adam was so awestruck by Eve's beauty that, upon first seeing her, he shouted, "Woe! Man!" and this is why Eve was called *woman*. OK, I clearly took some creative liberty there; what he actually said is, *"At last!...This one is bone from my bone, and flesh from my flesh! She will be called 'woman,' because she was taken from "man"'* (Gen. 2:23 NLT).

What we *do* know about humanity's first love match is that they experienced flawless companionship and unity. There was no fighting, griping, jealousy, or frustration, and no ongoing battles about whether the toilet seat should be left up or down. Suffice it to say, Adam and Eve complimented each other in a way that was quite literally *perfect*.

What can we learn about our female nature from Adam and Eve as it relates to love and attraction? For one, we were created to bring intimacy into a man's life, an intimacy that his work and productivity cannot possibly provide. I'm not saying that's our *only* purpose, but it is a God-designed female function nonetheless.

Second, we were designed to be adored by a man. Now this is *not* where we should derive our self-esteem or seek ultimate contentment. (I'll elaborate on this common mistake later.) I'm just pointing out that the first woman, Eve, was created to be valued as the object of Adam's affection, second only to God in Adam's life. Perhaps this is why so many little girls naturally dream of their wedding day and, as the years pass, fantasize about being swept off their feet by "the one."

I don't blame you if you are wondering why, if God created this spectacular dynamic between men and women, attraction and romance can be such a difficult thing to find these days—and even harder to maintain! Take Edward and Bella, for example. Even though in many ways they are the ultimate couple, they have their share of issues. Bella feels insecure and often questions why Edward wants to be with her. Edward conceals things from Bella at times and totally abandons her at one point. Like every couple, they have to work through miscommunications, and there are situations where they openly disagree. So if you think about it, even our "ideal couple" is not on cloud nine all of the time. As much as they desire to be together, Edward and Bella have struggles with their relationship.

The same is true for couples in real life of course, but once again, why? The answer to this question dates back to a liar, two rebels, and the cover of the *Twilight* book.

THE FALLOUT

It's remarkably chivalrous the way Edward is willing to put his life on the line to ensure that no wicked vampires harm his sweetheart, Bella. In *real* life, Adam stood by and did nothing when a "blood sucker" (satan) arrived on the garden scene to hurt Eve. (See Genesis 3.) Together, Adam and Eve willfully chose to rebel against God and partake of the *one thing* God asked them to refuse—fruit from a tree known as The Knowledge of Good and Evil. As you likely know, an apple is used as a modern day symbol of that "forbidden fruit." (Now you see why I mentioned the *Twilight* book cover, don't you?)

After Adam and Eve's "fall," everything changed, not just for Adam and Eve, but for every descendant thereafter. It was not only mankind's relationship with *God* that was severely damaged, but the effortless harmony between men and women took a devastating blow as well.

God was forthright about the consequences men and women would face as a result of Adam and Eve's rebellion and sin, and He explained to Eve, *"Your desire will be for your husband, and he will rule over you"* (Gen. 3:16). When studied in its original context, this passage of Scripture is saying that women will have an intrinsic desire to dominate their husbands and men will rule their wives with an iron fist—hardly the picture of romantic bliss Adam and Eve had formerly known.

So instead of using their brute strength for productivity and reserving their hearts for cherishing their mates, men started using their physical strength to dominate women while their hearts became more enthralled with work, conquests, and competitive feats (also known as videogame and sports addictions).

Instead of enjoying "Eve's" pursuit of intimate companionship, it's not uncommon for a modern-day man to get annoyed with his wife's ongoing desire for an emotional connection. In such cases, he prefers to spend the bulk of his down time preoccupied with entertainment or hobbies, perhaps gazing into his laptop and clutching the remote control as opposed to engaging in meaningful discussions with his wife. This is especially devastating to his wife because she recalls the "dating days" when he used to love nothing more than to hear the sound of her voice, and he hung on her every word.

"Eve" was created to bring relational intimacy into "Adam's" life, so naturally it's painful when he shuts her out.

Just in case you're getting the idea that it's only *men* who fell from perfection, allow me to tell you some common ways we women often error as a result of our fallen nature. Whereas Eve once served as Adam's greatest source of support and respect, we now struggle with the urge to degrade our male helpmates and compete with them for superiority (also known as the battle to "wear the pants"). As a general rule, women tend to manipulate by misusing our emotional wit to heap guilt and confusion on our not-so-emotionally-savvy male counterparts until we get our way. We can be overly sensitive, too critical and demanding at times, self-absorbed with how *we* feel, and, in many cases, obsessed with receiving ceaseless affection and attention from a man who, quite frankly, is growing weary of putting up with our moodiness and complaining. *Ouch!*

In summary, we know from Adam and Eve's rise and fall that men and women possess a strong, innate desire to be together and have the potential to bring immense joy and companionship to one another. But we also have a "fallen," self-centered nature that makes it nearly impossible for a couple to get along and remain attracted to each other for an extended length of time—especially "till death do us part!" So what's a girl to do?

Maybe we should do what Bella did and pick a *supernatural* man.

IF ONLY EDWARD WERE REAL—OR IS HE?

It's obvious why Bella is attracted to Edward. He's not only flawless in appearance; he's also selfless, brave, consistently gentle, and loyal. More importantly, he's super-human! He's not limited to the weaknesses of mere mortal men.

Now before you go dismissing that as pure fiction, consider this. While it's true that no man on earth can dart up and down trees with us riding on his back or appear as a mirage when we're about to get on the back of a rough dude's motorcycle, it *is* possible for a man to have a supernatural *nature*.

Check out this passage: *"If anyone is in Christ, he is a new creation; the old has gone, the new has come!"* (See 2 Cor. 5:17.)

A new creation? The old has gone? What does that really mean? Briefly stated, it means when Christ becomes our Savior, we get a new nature—God's all-loving nature. As a result, we can then live life out of this new, God-motivated nature and resist "fallen" attitudes and behaviors. As it pertains to a man committed to Christ, he has what it takes to treat "Eve" like the gift from God she's intended to be.

So get this. Remember how I just described the dominating, neglectful tendencies men took on after the fall? Well if a man is serving Christ, he will have *new* desires, desires that reflect the heart and nature of God. While he may be tempted to have those "fallen" attitudes at times, his devotion to Christ will ultimately lead him to treat a woman with love, servitude, and attentive devotion because, like Romans 8:9 says, he is not controlled by the sinful nature. In this way, he is unlike "mere mortals" and truly is a supernatural man. How cool is that?

Now please don't misunderstand me. I'm not saying that if we're with a Christ-loving man we'll never have conflict or moments when we feel so angry at him that we seriously consider making a throw pillow out of his favorite shirt. Men are different from us by God's design, and this creates conflict at times. In an upcoming chapter, we'll explore these differences with the intent of understanding and minimizing frustration. In the meantime, I want you to know that there truly are men out there who have renewed hearts, and, as a result, they treat women differently than the average "Joe." (If your honey's name is Joe, I'm not calling him average!)

We're told in Scripture not to be *"yoked together with unbelievers"* (2 Cor. 6:14). If we're not careful, we'll envision egg yoke and dismiss that passage as being too odd to ever practically apply to our lives. Our perspective changes a bit, however, when we realize that the "yoke" here is referring to the neck harness that binds two animals together, like oxen plowing a field, for example. So you see, God is warning us not to join our lives with a man who is not following Christ. This is not some snobby commandment that makes us "too good" for men of other faiths; this is practical advice to save us heartache down the road. A Christlike man is a supernatural man, and a supernatural man will treat us right. And God wants a man to treat us—to treat *you*—right!

HOW IS IT THAT SOME CHRISTIAN MEN DON'T ACT SUPERNATURAL?

When Bella meets Edward and starts getting to know him, she realizes there's something different about him, but she can't quite figure out what it is. Of course she doesn't suspect he's a vampire, but who can blame her for that? Initially, Edward does not tell Bella anything about his supernatural abilities, but as you well know, his super-human traits become obvious. Anytime a guy appears out of nowhere and stops an out-of-control car by simply putting his hand out, that's a strong indication that he's not exactly an everyday guy, right?

And so it is when you're looking for *your* supernatural guy. There are plenty of men out there who will talk about being a Christian. They may even go to church and have some Scriptures memorized, but this is not the totality of what we're looking for. Rather, we should observe the way he lives his life and keep our eyes open for signs that his faith is not just something he talks about but something he *lives* by. Just as Edward's supernatural abilities became obvious, in time, a man's supernatural nature (or lack thereof) will become obvious, too.

It's perfectly fine to come right out and ask a guy if he's a Christian. The danger is, upon hearing that he is a believer, assuming that this means he lives in obedient, passionate devotion to Christ. Once again, that's not to say that a man will be perfect just because he loves the Lord, but there's a significant difference between a guy who's just talking the talk and a man who's committed to walking the walk. As it pertains to Edward and the *Twilight* story, it's one thing for a guy to parade around like a vampire; it's another thing to really have been transformed into one. (I'm not promoting vampire rituals; just making a point.)

Perhaps you're married to a man who professes to be a Christian but in many ways, does not act like it, or he never even claimed to have a devotion to Christ in the first place. I've seen women get so angry about this that they give up on the marriage and seek a divorce, which I find ironic. They despise the fact that that their husband does not serve God with the same intensity they do, so they go out and do something *God* despises—they initiate a divorce (see Mal. 2:16). That's not to say that we should allow a man to abuse us; please don't misunderstand me! All I am saying is that if our husband is not behaving like a supernatural man, that's no excuse for us to abandon *our* call to behave like supernatural, Christlike women.

THE POWER TO MAKE SOMEONE MORE ATTRACTIVE

Bella can hardly wait to shed her fragile, aging humanity and become a stunning vampire, and the more she's around the Cullens, the more she wants to be transformed. There's something about this scenario I want to share with you that is applicable to our plight to ignite and maintain attraction, but it applies one way to married women and another way to singles.

FOR MY MARRIED SISTERS...

If you desire a more Christlike husband, I have great encouragement for you. Long before you were conceived, God knew you would be facing this challenge at this very point in your life. In His loving wisdom, He ensured that a certain passage of Scripture be included in the Bible that would speak directly to your situation. First Peter 3:1 is written to those of us whose husbands are not obeying the Word, whether they identify themselves as Christians or have never accepted Christ. The passage tells us what to do; *"...be submissive to your husbands so that, if any of them do not believe the word, they may be won over without words by the behavior of their wives."*

God is telling us to remain respectful, avoid "taking charge" of our husbands, even though we consider them spiritually weaker than us, and instead of nagging at them in hopes of generating change, model a life devoted to Christ. When we do this, the Holy Spirit comes along and ministers to our husband's heart in a way that far exceeds human abilities, wooing and leading him into a newfound respect and reverence, not only for us, but for God and His Word.

Just to clarify, when the Scripture speaks of winning over our husbands without words, this does not mean we are not at liberty to discuss marital issues with our spouse and share honest feelings with him. The principle the Scripture is conveying is that we don't have the power to change our husband, so rather than trying to talk him (or nag him) into becoming the man we want him to be, we should put our trust in Christ and trust *Him* to work on our husband's heart.

Living out First Peter 3:1 is certain to be a challenge and will no doubt take lots of patience, prayer, and supportive friends who build us up rather than discourage us and ridicule our husband. Nonetheless, the God of all creation has spoken and given us the secret to attracting our husbands, not only to us, but to God.

Just like Bella's exposure to Edward increases her desire to be *with* him and be *like* him, in time, our supernatural relationship with God can cause our husband to seek greater intimacy and connection with us and with Christ. Ultimately, our spouse has free will and God will not force him to do anything. Nonetheless, we must do our part and make an effort to do things God's way if we want to empower the Holy Spirit to work in our marriage.

Instead of complaining about all the things we wish our husband would do differently, what would happen if we spent that same time and energy interceding for him in prayer and relying on the Holy Spirit to help *us* be more attractive, more like Christ? It has been my experience on many occasions that I'm so fixated on what I consider to be my husband's shortcomings that I'm totally ignoring the character transformation the Holy Spirit is trying to bring about *in me*!

FOR MY SINGLE SISTERS...

Let's face it, Edward changes Bella. Her metamorphosis begins with feeling drawn to him, then she becomes infatuated with becoming a vampire just like him, until finally, the day comes when she is dramatically transformed. Ladies, we have to be careful with this scenario because, if we're not, we'll convince ourselves that *we too* have the power to transform the person we're dating.

I just finished sharing with married readers how, if their husbands are not serving God, there are instructions in the Bible for the right and wrong way to inspire change in them. However, the Scripture I encouraged them to read is for *married* people, not dating or engaged couples! I've already mentioned God's instruction for singles—He warns us *not* to become entangled in the first place with a man who isn't seeking Christ (see 2 Cor. 6:14). It's one thing to realize we've violated God's standards after we've said "I do." It's another thing to ignore God's warning, get married, then go to God for help because our spouse isn't changing like we thought he would.

Females with a big heart often latch onto guys who are simply not in the right place spiritually. They may be nice guys who identify themselves as Christians, yet lack a meaningful devotion to

Christ and tend to compromise Biblical standards. Then again, they may be not-so-nice, openly defiant toward Christ, and struggling with destructive attitudes and behaviors. With good intentions, a girlfriend will come along and try to transform him into a Christlike *supernatural*-natured man. This is a real problem, however, because *dating and courtship is not about changing a man into what we want him to be; it's about finding that one guy who **already is** the godly man we need him to be.*

WHAT GUYS FIND *UNATTRACTIVE:*

As enthralled as Edward is with Bella, I asked some guys if they think Bella's personality is attractive, and surprisingly, most of them said no. Here are a few of the reasons they cited:

- She's too insecure.
- She rarely smiles and has no sense of humor.
- She has no life of her own. Guys don't like to be a girl's only interest.
- She's just kind of there; there's nothing about her personality that would get my attention.
- She gets depressed too easily.

Trying to rehabilitate or bring spiritual revival to someone we're dating is referred to as "missionary dating," and in my book for singles, *Why Wait*, I discuss the dangers of this in more detail. For now, suffice it to say, if you're dating or engaged to someone whom you find yourself coaching along, bailing out, preaching to, or making excuses for his bad behavior, you need to heed God's warning and bring closure to that romantic relationship. I know that's not at all what you want to hear, but it's true. And if you feel like his life will spiral out of control if you break up with him, that's all the more reason to end it. You're *not* his Savior; Christ is!

MORE ABOUT ATTRACTION

While it's always good to take care of our physical appearance, the source of mutual attraction goes far beyond a man's dazzling smile or a woman's Brazilian tan—and it certainly transcends our bra size! A key to attraction that many people overlook is *respect*. The more respect a couple shows each other, the more passion, sizzle, and physical desire they will feel for one another, even as the years go by. This is why, when we're married, our spiritual enemy works so hard to try and convince us that our spouse isn't worthy of our respect. He begins whispering in our ear, "Your husband doesn't deserve your loyalty and respect. You need something else to make you happy... *someone* else." Ironically, that's the same sort of lie he told Adam and Eve about God.

There is no one more worthy of respect than Jesus Christ, so that's why we should seek to be like Him and hold out for a man who seeks Christ-likeness as well. Whether you're praying to meet that supernatural man you're going to marry or you're praying for the man you married to be more supernatural, may I lovingly encourage you to *do things God's way*. Follow His principles and scriptural instructions. And remember *to whom* you are praying – to God, the very one who invented attraction and romantic chemistry in the first place.

This book, including the *Reflections on Romance* questions, will hopefully get you thinking about love and romance, but how do we know if we're thinking about it too much? More to the point, does our life revolve around a man, or the hope of finding one? How can we find balance? I cannot wait to explore this topic with you in the next chapter!

REFLECTIONS ON ROMANCE—CHAPTER 2

1. Are you aware of some differences between the way a man devoted to Christ treats a woman versus a man who does not follow Christ? List some of the differences.

_____

_____

_____

_____

2. If you are single, how committed are you to avoiding being "unequally yoked" with a man? If you are married, how committed are you to following First Peter 3:1?

_____

_____

_____

_____

3. Are you currently, or have you ever been, involved in a missionary dating situation? What are the excuses we use to stay in the relationship, and how can these be overcome?

_____

_____

_____

_____

_____

_____

4. What are some practical ways you can show respect to the current or future man in your life?

_____

_____

_____

_____

_____

5. What's the one thing that spoke to you the most in this chapter, and why?

_____

_____

_____

_____

_____

PRAYER

While our society focuses almost entirely on physical appearance as a means of igniting and maintaining attraction, help me, Lord, to remember that your Kingdom principles operate differently. Beautify me on the inside. Make me more Christlike. Cultivate a tender heart in my [future] husband that seeks to please You. Help him to hunger and thirst for righteousness, and give him revelation he may be lacking when it comes to loving and honoring me as his wife and You as his Lord. Knit our hearts together and help us maintain mutual attraction and respect for one another, even on those days when we fall short of Your perfect standards. Most importantly, help me to maintain respect for You and honor You through obedience to Your Word. In Jesus' name, amen.

Endnote

1. Stephenie Meyer, *Twilight* (New York: Hachette Book Group USA, 2005), 22.

Chapter Three

BALANCED

 Does my life revolve around "Edward"?

My heart aches for Bella. An extraordinary guy comes along, stirs her heart into a love-struck frenzy, and leads her to believe she's found lasting romance. Then he tells her he never wants to see her again and, quite literally, disappears. Confused and devastated, Bella sinks into a dark depression. While trapped in an emotional black hole, she could care less about friends, social functions, school, her future—anything really. She just wants Edward back.

I remember feeling dizzy during the movie *New Moon* as the camera circles Bella, slumped over in utter defeat, and we witness the seasons change while her depression remains. It's only when she starts visiting with Jacob that her emotional forecast begins to change. As she spends her days with him, the rain clouds part and her soul warms up to the sunlight again.

Can you identify with Bella? Have you ever felt the sting of rejection or the pain of lost love? Has a man you trusted ever shocked you with betrayal? Do you know what it's like for the one who used to adore you to now ignore you? Maybe you have yet to experience romantic affection in the first place, but your heart desperately longs for it. No matter the case, you are not alone. There are multitudes of women out there asking, *Where's my Edward? When will the sun shine on me?*

THE SUN

It's hard to believe that the earth is 98.52 *million* miles away from the sun, and yet our lives are sustained by its light and heat. Not only that, the sun is what keeps the earth from floating off into the deadness of outer space. Our planet maintains a constant orbit around the sun at a mindboggling speed of 67,000 miles per hour! As we revolve around our solar system's largest star—the sun—our planet is stabilized and secure.

What do *you* rely on for stability? What is it that enables you to keep your emotions intact, and to where do you look for security? What—or *who*—does your life revolve around?

Whether you know the answer to those questions or not, I assure you, there's something you depend on as a source of contentment and joy. It may be an active social life, extracurricular achievements, acceptance and admiration from your peers, an ongoing accumulation of material possessions, or dreams of future success. Perhaps it is your relationship with Christ. Then again, it could be an infatuation with love and romance that motivates your soul day after day. If that's the case, I think it's fair to say that your life revolves around "Edward"—the guy in your life or the hope of having a guy in your life.

For Bella, Edward is most certainly essential for her personal happiness, and I can identify. As stated in a previous chapter, my father's absence led me to an unrealistic idea about having a man by my side. I honestly believed if I could fall in love and get married, I would finally find the happiness my dissatisfied soul had craved for as long as I could remember. And so the cycle began. I would search with all of my energy for a love match, then invest everything I had in a dating relationship, honestly believe it was leading to marriage, only to experience a painful breakup, mourn, then roll up my tearstained sleeves and start all over again searching with all of my energy for a love match. Like Bella, the only thing that cheered me up after losing an

"Edward" was meeting a "Jacob"—another guy who was interested in me.

Eventually, my reasoning mind got a hold of my runaway emotions and I connected the scattered dots of my dysfunctional love life. While the desire to love and be loved by a man was a good, even God-given yearning, it was never meant to become an infatuation that my life revolved around. Unlike the sun, which was created to sustain and stabilize the earth, a man—even a *godly* man—is not capable of sustaining my happiness or stabilizing my life.

In my desire to find and secure a life partner, I had actually crossed over into *idolatry*, which is to say, my plight to experience a love connection overshadowed my passion and dependence on God. I prioritized romantic relationships over my relationship with Christ, which was how my life became seriously out of balance and why I grew increasingly unhappy. It was easy to *say* serving Christ was my top priority, but my thoughts, heart's desires, and daily focus revealed otherwise.

Do you know what causes depression? *We get depressed when our source of joy and contentment lets us down.* While it's true that hormonal fluctuations and imbalances can cause us to feel depressed, it is often the case that our feelings of sadness, hopelessness, and disillusionment are the end-result of having entrusted our life's happiness to something or someone that failed to meet our expectations (Hence Bella's utter depression when Edward left).

If, like me, you find yourself believing that you will never be discontent again if you could just meet the right man, marry your boyfriend, or see your husband finally make some desired changes, allow me to lovingly point out that this is simply *not* true. While there is joy associated with meeting "the one," marrying a great guy, or having our husband turn over a new leaf or two, there's only *one source* worthy and capable to be the "sun" in our lives, and that's *the Son*, Jesus Christ.

BASKING IN THE SON'S LIGHT

Perhaps you wonder how Jesus can satisfy you when He's no longer even here on earth. You want something tangible to look to for contentment on a daily basis, not mere spiritual theories or principles. If that's your heart's cry, I hear you, sister! Through tears of frustration, I used to beg God to explain to me how in the world I'm supposed to esteem Him as my heart's top priority. I can't even see Him; how could He ever satisfy my longing soul?

Once again, we look to the sun as a means of comparison. I don't walk outside and physically stare at the sun everyday—that would hurt my eyes! Instead, when I walk outside, I feel the sun's heat. Furthermore, while I do not see my skin change instantly, if I stay in the sun long enough, my darkened pigment will testify that I truly did absorb some rays. And on days when it's freezing or rain clouds have drowned out the sun, all that means is that certain factors are blocking the sun's heat and rays; the sun is still there, shining bright like always.

And so it is with God. We don't see Him, but we can feel the Holy Spirit's presence at times, warming our heart when our soul is suffering from life's cold circumstances. Just like we have to turn off the television and go outside if we want to bask in the sunlight, we have to make a consistent effort to get away from life's many distractions and get into God's presence through prayer. Now when I say *prayer*, I'm not referring to some formal, eloquent means of expression to God, but rather, a sincere, "here's what I'm thankful for and what I need Your help with" kind of communication with our heavenly Father. Even though we don't see our prayers "working" in that moment, in time, we will see our lives transform, experience a meaningful connection with God, and ultimately witness our prayer life yield results. These experiences accumulate and, before you know it, we find God to be an ever-present friend, invisible, yet always there for us in a way that exceeds the abilities of our friends, family, boyfriend, or husband. It's not that we cease to need others in our lives; it's just that our lives don't revolve around them. (If only Bella understood this!)

Undeveloped, uneducated cultures often make assumptions about the sun—it's the eyeball of a mystic bird; it's a window into eternal paradise; it's the sun god who gets angry unless 10 ears of corn are offered as a daily sacrifice. A study of the sun, however, reveals it's actually a ball of hot gasses—not exactly something we want to present with sacrificial corn offerings. In a similar fashion, if we're not careful, we'll make up ideas about God that aren't true. "God expects me to be perfect." "God would never punish a nation for behaving wickedly." "Christ is *one* way to Heaven, but not the only way." Biblically speaking, all of those statements are false, but if we don't study and learn what the Bible reveals about God, we will be inclined to believe things that aren't true and miss out on the many wonders about God that *are* true.

Sometimes life gets cloudy and we don't feel the *Son's* warmth like we would like, but just as the sun is always there shining bright above the storm, we can trust that God is always there too. He is not only there; He is beckoning us to entrust Him with our life's happiness. Even though He primarily operates outside the realm of our five senses, He is well able to provide us with all the peace, joy, contentment, and stability we need. It's hard to believe, but then again, so are the facts about the sun!

It took me years to realize that, like Bella, while I was attempting to make a man the *sun* in my life, he was supposed to be the *moon*...

MEN ARE LIKE MOONS

I think a moonlit night can be very romantic. What's interesting is that the moon does not generate light. It may look like a celestial light bulb, but in actuality, the moon is merely reflecting the sun's light to the earth. Furthermore, the earth and the moon revolve around the sun together, and the moon only shines to the degree that the sun shines on it.

How are men like moons? Well, rather than our lives revolving around them, our life is meant to be joined with a man who will revolve around the *Son* with us, as a couple united by a common love for Christ. And while a man does not generate his own spiritual light, the light of Christ that shines on Him will ultimately reflect and shine on us. He experiences God's goodness (also known as God's *glory*); therefore, he is good to us. This is what First Corinthians 11:7 is referring to when it says man is the glory of God, and woman is the glory of man.

The imagery of a new moon and eclipse that Stephenie Myer uses for two of the books in her *Twilight* series is quite interesting. A new moon is actually an eclipse that occurs when the moon stands directly between the earth and the sun. (Do you have a mental picture of that?) As a result, the moon becomes almost totally invisible from earth and is unable to reflect the sun's light back to us, which makes for an extremely dark night.

Ladies, are we guilty of letting a guy stand between Christ and us? Is a romantic infatuation blocking Christ's joy-sustaining light in our lives? If so, we can expect some dark nights ahead. On the other hand, nothing lights up a dark night like *true* love!

TRUE LOVE VERSUS INFATUATION

It's commonly said that love is blind. I totally disagree with that idea. It's not *love* that's blind, but rather, *infatuation*. While the definition of love varies from one person to the next, the Bible sets the precedence and describes love this way:

> *Love is patient...*
> http://www.biblestudytools.com/1-corinthians/13
> .html-cr-descriptionAnchor-9

> *...love is kind. It does not envy, it does not boast, it is not proud....*
> http://www.biblestudytools.com/1-corinthians/13
> .html-cr-descriptionAnchor-10

...It is not rude, it is not self-seeking,...
http://www.biblestudytools.com/1-corinthians/13
.html-cr-descriptionAnchor-11

...it is not easily angered,...
http://www.biblestudytools.com/1-corinthians/13
.html-cr-descriptionAnchor-12

...it keeps no record of wrongs....
http://www.biblestudytools.com/1-corinthians/13
.html-cr-descriptionAnchor-13

...Love does not delight in evil...
http://www.biblestudytools.com/1-corinthians/13
.html-cr-descriptionAnchor-14

...but rejoices with the truth....
http://www.biblestudytools.com/1-corinthians/13
.html-cr-descriptionAnchor-15

*...It always protects, always trusts, always
hopes, always perseveres....*
http://www.biblestudytools.com/1-corinthians/13
.html-cr-descriptionAnchor-16

...Love never fails (1 Corinthians 13:4-8).

According to that definition, nothing is more clear-sighted than love! Look over that biblical description again. To love a man is to be acquainted with his shortcomings. Why else would we need to be patient, resist easily becoming angered, and leave previous wrongs in the past? As it pertains to marriage, to love with a God-kind of love is to know who a man truly is—abilities and faults, strengths and weaknesses, freshly shaved and bed-head—and determine to honor and cherish him anyway while we work through relational challenges.

Infatuation is quite the opposite of love. When we're infatuated with a guy, we *only* see the good. If friends or loved ones try to point out areas of his behavior that warrant concern, we are defensive and refuse to objectively consider his faults. Should we happen to observe something about him we seriously don't like, we either make excuses for him or try to change him. (If you recall, in the last chapter we touched on the problems this creates.)

Infatuation is based on the false belief that we need to be in a certain relationship in order to maintain our own personal happiness (i.e., he's "the sun" our lives revolve around). As a result, we shun anything that threatens the relationship.

Infatuations are usually breeding grounds for jealousy. Whereas *love* is based on trust, an infatuated couple is plagued by ongoing suspicions, worries, and insecurities.

We may *think* we're in love with a guy, when in actuality, we're in love with the idea of having a man in our life. The problem is that if we get married based on infatuation, and in time he no longer makes us *feel* the way he did before, we'll conclude that we've fallen out of love with him. In reality, we never *loved* him in the first place, not according to the Bible's definition.

Make no mistake about it; *love is a decision, not an emotion.* Yes, emotions are involved, but by their very nature, emotions are inconsistent and come and go. Conversely, love is an unwavering commitment. Look back at the Scriptural definition of love. Are there any *feelings* mentioned? No. Instead we're given a description of godly *attitudes* and *actions.*

Infatuation is based almost entirely on feelings and more specifically, feelings of fear. We fear being without a guy for one reason or another. Consider Bella's words when Edward leaves, *"Love, life, meaning...over."*[2] Bella is *afraid* to face life without her boyfriend.

Our motivation for staying in an infatuation-based dating relationship centers around our *own* desires for our *own* life. "I don't want to be alone." "I want my friends to see and admire my relationship." "I want out of my parents' house." "I want to be happy, and I will be if I could just get married." These are all foundations on which infatuations are built, and *none* of them has *anything* to do with truly loving a man.

In actuality, emotions tend to follow actions, which is why when we determine to *act* on the biblical definition of love, in time, we tend to *feel* more love. Now before you go assuming I'm advocating a robotic approach to love, let's talk about the role emotions *do* play.

ONE MORE THING ABOUT LOVE, MEN, AND THE MOON

Did you know that the moon directly affects the ocean's tides? I find that amazing! Along those lines, while we do not want our lives to revolve around a man, genuinely loving a man *will* require giving him access to the intimate tides of our heart. In this way, we become vulnerable to the man we love. Furthermore, there's no need to apologize then when we feel a strong sense of attachment to a man, nor is it "unspiritual" to desire greater emotional chemistry within marriage.

A friend of mine once commented, "Emotions are like toddlers; they are sweet and fun to have around, but have no business being put in charge!" And so it is with our emotions in regard to romance. We should enjoy our feelings and pay attention to what they are telling us while also seeking perspective about our love relationship in a way that transcends mere emotion.

Love and vulnerability are inseparably connected. If "Edward" pursues and adores us, our heart soars. If "Edward" leaves, we're going to hurt. However, if our lives revolve around the *Son*, the difference between

Bella and us is that "Edward's" absence can *hurt* us, but it will not *destroy* us and leave us emotionally destitute until a new man comes along. Nonetheless, like Bella, we have to be willing to take a risk and surrender our hearts to love; the key is knowing *when* and to *whom*. This is the all-important topic of our next chapter!

REFLECTIONS ON ROMANCE—CHAPTER 3

1. Take an honest inventory and consider what you rely on as a source of contentment and satisfaction; write those things down, then answer the question, Are these things working?

    _____

    _____

    _____

    _____

2. Do you fear being without a man? (If you are married, did you fear being without a man when you were single?) Why or why not?

    _____

    _____

    _____

    _____

3. Have you ever truly looked to Jesus as your life's primary focus and source of satisfaction? What challenges have you experienced or do you anticipate as you try to do this?

    _____

_____

_____

_____

4. What are some practical ways at this time in your life you could learn more about God and the Bible? (e.g., attend a Bible study, take your questions to a knowledgeable person, etc.) How might you go about actually doing this versus just thinking about it?

_____

_____

_____

_____

_____

5. What are your thoughts about love versus infatuation, and how does that concept apply to your life right now?

_____

_____

_____

_____

PRAYER

Father, I know that because You love me, you have commanded me to turn away from idolatry. Forgive me for looking to people or things to satisfy me when You clearly desire to have first place in my heart and serve as the anchor for my soul. Show me how to walk with You even though You operate beyond my five senses. Help me to be vulnerable with You and confide in You while also doing my part to learn about You and Your Word. As my heart longs for lasting romance, keep me balanced. Holy Spirit, convict me and draw me close to You when I am looking to satisfy my heart at the expense of my relationship with Christ. In Jesus' name I pray, amen.

Endnotes

1. Stephenie Meyer, *New Moon* (New York: Hachette Book Group USA, 2006), 72.
2. *Ibid.*

Chapter Four

CHERISHED

Are my standards high enough?

*Edward regards Bella with the utmost respect and adoration. I recently spoke with some high school girls, however, who had a totally different experience with the guys in their lives. I was invited to facilitate a discussion during their second period parenting class, which was exclusively for teen moms. I've carried on conversations with young girls about sex and dating on many occasions, but this day was drastically different. Whereas girls are usually bright-eyed, giggly, and downright elated at the thought of falling in love, these young women sat there expressionless, skeptical at the mere mention of the word **love**. Their dreams of having a **Twilight**-kind of romance had long been shattered by the nightmarish reality of their life experiences. At one time, they sincerely believed they were cherished by a guy; how painful to awaken to the reality that they were actually a casualty of his lust and betrayal.*

Their disappointment, hopelessness, and resentment hovered in the room like a smothering fog.

These girls not only had wounds from their past but had clearly given up on having higher expectations for the future. In their minds, this was all a young woman could expect from a man. There would never be a handsome prince willing to fight for them. No fairy tale ending awaiting the next season of their lives. They believed that the best they could do was give their bodies to guys in hopes that they would someday reciprocate with some amount of respect and commitment. For these girls, the notion of being cherished and adored by an "Edward" was a farfetched hope not worthy of even considering.

Oh, how amazing it was to shine some light on their dark perspectives! As I spoke that day, it became abundantly clear that they were not aware that they had a *right* to expect more from a man. More to the point, these young ladies had never considered their own personal worth. They had no idea that they were *far too valuable* to be used or abused by a guy. Upon hearing these truths, the girls sat up straighter in their chairs, unfolded their arms, and even began to smile.

"You mean I don't *have* to have sex with a guy? I can wait until a man loves and cares for me enough to marry me? I don't *have* to put up with name calling, unfaithfulness, and fits of anger?"

Like a bird escaping the death grip of a trap, the news that they were worthy of higher standards was profoundly liberating for them. Still, when I left, my heart was heavy. I knew that they took my encouragement to heart, but I also realized that, as human beings, we tend to fall right back into our same old behaviors, expectations, and life patterns. I prayed that God would continue to solidify His standards in their hearts and send more people across their paths to remind them that they *don't* have to settle for an unhealthy love relationship.

EDWARD'S EXAMPLE

While there's no such thing as the perfect man, there are gentlemen out there. No, they are not a dime a dozen, but they *do* exist. In the *Twilight* storyline there are noble vampires and cruel vampires, and so it is in life—there are *great* guys and *ape* guys. Great guys are those who know how to honor and respect a woman; ape guys are those who initially appear strong and cuddly, but if we get too close, they will instinctively hurt us.

As we consider how we deserve to be treated, why don't we look at how *Twilight's* most valiant character regards the woman in his life? I'm talking about Edward, of course. Say what you want about his pale, icy skin—the guy knows how to treat a woman!

Edward never hurts Bella, but rather, protects her.

For me, one of the most attractive qualities about Edward is that he is so concerned with protecting Bella. Furthermore, he is the *last* person who would ever want to wound or harm her. He'd rather die than see her suffer.

Hopefully you have already come to this conclusion yourself: *no man has a right to physically hurt you.* There are some things about a man we can live with—physical abuse is *not* one of them.

It can seem perplexing at times when a girl, or a grown woman for that matter, keeps going back to a man who abuses her, but it's most often because there's an odd dynamic at work. You see, after he attacks her, his countenance drastically softens and he returns to her with great sorrow. He will usually attempt to comfort her in the midst of her physical, emotional, and mental anguish. This is confusing for a woman because the same man is filling two opposing roles in her life—he's the one who beats her, but he's also the one who "rescues" her afterward during moments of utter despair. The key is to turn on the ole' light bulb in our noggins and realize that we wouldn't *need* his comfort if he wasn't abusing us!

"Perhaps he will change someday," women tell themselves. To that I say, "Good, maybe he'll treat the *next* woman right, because *I'm* sure not willing to stay with him!" It is not our job to serve as the proverbial guinea pig in an abusive man's life—allowing the measure of his rehabilitation to be tested on our body and soul.

Edward Is a Man of His Word

If we're going to give our heart to a man, it needs to be a man whom we can count on. Furthermore, when a man consistently does what he says he will do, it builds trust. If you think about it, Edward does not lie to Bella about where he's been, what he's been doing, or who he is spending time with. If he says he's going to meet her somewhere or do something for her, he does it. We have a right to expect this from the man in our life as well.

If you find that the guy you're dating is not upfront and honest with you, then he is failing in the area of dependability. Now don't go accusing him of keeping secrets when, in actuality, you are far too "up in his business" and paranoid. He shouldn't have to text you and tell you his whereabouts every five minutes. Having said that, if, after he tells you he's going to handle something or do something, you find yourself thinking, "Yah, right," based on times past when he has let you down, that's not a good sign.

Edward Never Speaks Harshly or Disrespectfully to Bella

Edward sets such a fantastic example of how we should expect a man to talk to us. Although most guys are not going to be nearly as poetic or eloquent with their words of affection as Edward, the important thing is that their tone and words are affirming and soothing, not scary and degrading.

We talked about physical abuse, but what about verbal cruelty? If a man is calling you names, cursing at you, or saying things with the intent of hurting you, that is abuse; it just leaves *emotional* scars as opposed to physical wounds. No matter how stressed he is, how mad he says *we* made him, or how he tries to justify his verbal assaults, you and I are never to serve as an emotional punching bag for a man. If he's got pent up anger, he needs to take it out somewhere else.

If you are married to a verbally abusive man, you need to seek qualified, wise third-party counsel immediately! If your boyfriend is a verbal abuser, you need to be boyfriend-less by this time tomorrow. Seriously!

Edward Loves Bella With a Balanced Jealousy

Jealousy is a concept that is often confused. There is such thing as *healthy* jealousy. For example, I love my husband, and if I saw him carrying on a flirtatious conversation with another woman, it would naturally provoke a protective jealousy in me. Moreover, God describes Himself as a jealous God, meaning He loves us, longs for our time and attention, and His protectiveness is provoked when we give our highest devotion to anything other than Him (see Exod. 34:14).

Then there's *unhealthy* jealousy. This is not motivated by love, but by insecurity and fear. A guy feels so inferior about himself that he worries his girl is going to leave him for someone else. As a result, he is constantly falsely accusing her of looking at guys and cheating. No matter how irrational his suspicions are or how much we present the truth, a guy motivated by an unhealthy jealousy will not believe us.

Think marrying him will make things better? Wrong! There's nothing you can do to prove to a jealous man you are *not* untrustworthy. He needs inner healing and counseling, not more commitment from you.

While Edward does get concerned when he suspects Bella may be putting herself in harm's way, he does not dictate where she goes, who she hangs around, or accuse her of looking at other guys.

At the risk of sounding like a broken record, if you're married to a man who has unhealthy jealous tendencies, you need to seek counsel right away. If you're dating a jealous guy, quit trying to prove your love for him and let him go. I know you feel like, in doing so, you are confirming what he's believed all along (that you would leave him). But a relationship must have trust to succeed, so there's no sense in continuing to put up with his unfair "drama" and false accusations.

Edward Is Faithful

I find great significance in the fact that Edward has only fallen in love with *one* woman. Even a century before Bella was born, there was never a woman who captivated his heart the way she does. We'll look at this dynamic in greater detail in an upcoming chapter, but for now, the important thing is that we realize a *good* man is a *faithful* man.

Our culture and the mainstream media are selling men a lie. They act like the more women a guy "conquers" sexually, the more manly he is. Of course this is not true. Any dog can go out and mate with multiple partners, but it takes a *real* man to overcome lust and respect his monogamous commitment.

I'm not going to belabor this point. If you don't trust the guy you're with to behave himself around other females when you're not around, that's a huge red flag that he's not the one for you. If you're dating a guy who's always gawking at other girls and flirting, realize that for what it is—he's not ready to "forsake all others" and become an exclusive partner with you.

And while there are some differences between a guy looking at pornography versus actually going out and having sex with a girl, the differences are pure technicalities when it comes to faithfulness. A boyfriend or husband who is into pornography is not being faithful to the woman in his life.

What do you think I'm going to say next? Right! If you're married to an unfaithful man, seek qualified counsel right away. If you're dating one, don't bother trying to take the relationship any further. He can't be trusted, and you deserve better.

Edward Respects Bella Sexually

This point is so important that I've written an entire upcoming chapter about it. In the meantime, let me just say that if a guy is putting sexual pressure on you, he is disrespecting you. It may not feel like disrespect—it may feel like you're gorgeous and he is enthralled by your beauty. But in reality, he is esteeming his own sexual gratification above your value and worth. Once again, you deserve better.

That's all I'm going to say about that...*for now!*

"BUT I LOVE HIM!"

When encouraging a female to break it off with an abusive man, it is not uncommon for her to say, "But

I love him," as if that somehow trumps all common sense and makes it reasonable to stay with him. Based on material from the last chapter, a woman who stays with an abusive man is actually *infatuated* with him as opposed to being in love with him. She *fears* living without him for one reason or another.

It's not loving to put up with abuse—*it's enabling*. When we maintain a romantic relationship with an abusive man, we *allow* him to remain an abuser. Ladies, if we don't love *ourselves* enough to seek protection and stay out of harm's way, there's no way we can properly love someone else. Moreover, using "love" as justification to stay with an abusive man is a serious contradiction. Love has standards!

There's no one who loves humanity more than God, and you know what He has to say to abusers? God warns men that if they deal treacherously with their wives, He will not answer their prayers or receive their praise (see Mal. 2:13-14). If God, who literally *is* love, has standards regarding how a man treats a woman, shouldn't we?

And as a final point, let's pay attention to our friends and loved ones should they express concern about the way we're being treated. If we find ourselves growing more and more isolated from them, that is a serious wake-up call that something is wrong.

HOW THE OTHER HALF LIVES

Up to this point, we've focused almost exclusively on our female desires, standards, and tendencies as it pertains to love and romance. But what about the other half of the world's population? How do *guys* feel about love and romance? In the next chapter, we'll explore the masculine perspective and get a reliable answer to the question, "Will a man ever love me the way Edward loves Bella?"

First, take a moment to answer the *Reflections on Romance* questions and express the guided prayer to the Lord. Then, if you are currently dating someone or married, take the following quiz and see how your relationship measures up.

REFLECTIONS ON ROMANCE—CHAPTER 4

1. What do you admire most about the way Edward treats Bella?

    _____

    _____

    _____

    _____

    _____

2. In reviewing the standards listed in the chapter, are you currently (or have you ever been) in a relationship where one or more of those standards is/was violated? If so, explain the experience and why you deserve better.

    _____

    _____

    _____

    _____

    _____

3. Why is it a wrong application of love for a woman to stay with an abusive man "because she loves him"? Why is it

important to heed the concern of friends and loved ones?

_____

_____

_____

_____

4. As we transition to the next chapter, what do you find the most perplexing about men as it relates to love and romance?

_____

_____

_____

_____

_____

_____

PRAYER

If married...

Father, I am Your daughter, a treasured object of Your affection. Please help me to set and maintain standards that reflect Your will for my life. Give me wisdom and discernment as I relate to my husband, and show me what boundaries are necessary. I ask that you impress upon my husband's heart the importance of treating me with honor and respect. Please surround him with men who love and esteem their wives, and, if necessary, lead us to the third-party counsel we need in order to bring about change in our marriage. Thank you for not only hearing my prayer, but answering. In Jesus' name I pray, amen.

If single, dating, or engaged...

Father, I am Your daughter, a treasured object of your affection. Please help me to set and maintain standards that reflect Your will for my life. Give me wisdom and discernment as I relate to the opposite sex, and show me what boundaries are needed. If am currently involved, or become involved in the future, with a man who does not honor and esteem me the way You intend, give me the strength and courage to end that relationship. Lord, I give You my word that I will not isolate myself from friends and loved ones, but will instead heed their apprehensions should they express concern about my relationship. Thank you for not only hearing my prayer, but answering. In Jesus' name I pray, amen.

IS MY RELATIONSHIP HEALTHY?

SECTION ONE

Put a check if you and your boyfriend/spouse...

- ☐ Have fun together most of the time.
- ☐ Each enjoy spending time separately with your own friends, as well as with each other's friends.
- ☐ Always feel safe with each other.
- ☐ Trust each other.
- ☐ Are faithful to each other (if you have made this commitment).
- ☐ Support each other's individual goals in life, like ministry, education, or career goals.
- ☐ Respect each other's opinions, even when they are different.
- ☐ Solve conflicts without putting each other down, cursing at each other, or making threats.
- ☐ Enjoy spiritually beneficial conversations that center around the truth of God's Word.
- ☐ Both accept responsibility for your actions.
- ☐ Both apologize when you're wrong.
- ☐ Both have decision-making power in the relationship.

☐ Are proud to be with each other.

☐ Encourage each other's interests like sports and leisure activities.

☐ Have some privacy—your letters, journals, and personal phone calls are respected as your own.

☐ Have close friends and relatives who are happy about your relationship.

☐ Never feel like you're being pressured for sex.

☐ Always allow each other "space" when you need it.

☐ Always treat each other with respect.

SECTION TWO

Put a check if **one** *of you...*

☐ Gets extremely jealous or accuses the other of cheating or wanting to cheat.

☐ Puts the other down by calling names, cursing, or making the other feel bad about him or herself.

☐ Yells or speaks in harsh tones.

☐ Doesn't take the other person, or things that are important to him/her, seriously.

☐ Doesn't respect the other person when he/she talks.

☐ Frequently criticizes the other's friends or family.

☐ Pressures the other for sex.

☐ Has ever threatened to hurt the other or commit suicide if the other leaves.

☐ Cheats or threatens to cheat.

☐ Is into pornography.

☐ Dictates how the other person dresses.

☐ Is opposed to or makes fun of the other's commitment to Christ or involvement with church.

☐ Acts one way at church but another way outside of church.

☐ Has ever grabbed, pushed, hit, or physically hurt the other.

☐ Blames the other for his or her own behavior ("If you hadn't made me mad, I wouldn't have…").

☐ Embarrasses or humiliates the other.

☐ Smashes, throws, or destroys things.

☐ Tries to keep the other from having commitments and ambitions, such as a job or education goals.

☐ Makes all the decisions about what the two of you do.

☐ Tries to make the other feel crazy or plays mind games.

☐ Goes back on promises and regularly does not keep his/her word.

☐ Acts controlling or possessive.

☐ Uses alcohol or drugs.

☐ Ignores or withholds affection as a way of punishing the other.

☐ Depends completely on the other to meet social or emotional needs.

SCORING

Multiple checks in Section One and no checks in Section Two:

It seems that your relationship has healthy qualities. If you are dating and the relationship continues for another three months, take the quiz again and see if the results have changed any.

One or more checks in Section Two:

You need to immediately seek input from a qualified third-party source concerning your relationship. It appears to be lacking the qualities of a healthy relationship and has the potential to be harmful to you. Please take this warning seriously!

Unhealthy dating and marital relationships are not something to ignore.

Endnote

1. Stephenie Meyer, *Eclipse* (New York: Hachette Book Group USA, 2007).

Chapter Five

ENLIGHTENED

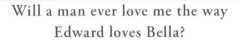

Will a man ever love me the way
Edward loves Bella?

*Edward's intoxicating adoration for Bella beckons
each of us to ask, Will a man ever love me that
way? Will a man and I want each other—****forever?***
*As we seek to answer these questions, we must look
beyond* Twilight's *leading heartthrob and consider
how* ***real*** *men define and express love.*

A DISTORTED VIEW OF THE OPPOSITE SEX

A male friend of mine shared the following obser-
vation, and I think it merits now sharing with you. He
explained that, while there are numerous repercussions
men experience as a result of pornography addictions,
one devastating consequence is an inevitable distorted
view of women. Pornography is the end result of make-
believe, strategically staged sexual encounters, meaning

that the women involved are doing sexual acts, not because they find it fulfilling, but rather, to meet the photographer or movie director's expectations. They fill a role; they get paid. Furthermore, the way women talk and behave in pornographic settings does *not* likely reflect the average woman's love-making desires.

While a carnal, lustful man is thrilled to see women revel in perversion and loveless sex, chances are his wife's sexual standards and preferences are nothing like a porn star's performances! Even if a man is married to a confident lady who enjoys seducing him and satisfying his physical desires, his preoccupation with farfetched extreme perversion will sabotage arousal toward his wife. After all, she doesn't talk dirty, dress trashy, or push sexual boundaries like the women featured in pornography. (Perhaps this is why so many men today complain of sexual performance challenges.)

I'm sure you have already come to this conclusion: It's not fair for men to compare their significant other to the females in pornography—or even to digitally enhanced women in movies or magazines.

Believe it or not, ladies, this is where we might be guilty of hypocrisy. Just like females in pornography do not represent what women really want and have to offer their mate sexually, Hollywood hunks featured in onscreen love stories rarely portray what the average man wants and has to offer a woman *emotionally*. The leading men in romance novels and movies are breathtakingly poetic and incredibly sensitive, yet tough enough to rescue their female costars from danger *every time,* no matter what feats of strength are required. Of course these men are not real—they are characters fulfilling a role developed in the minds of creative, talented people.

Do you see where I'm going with this? Just like men have to guard their eyes against illicit images that distort their view and expectations of women, we have to guard our hearts against unrealistic, fictitious ideas of men that cause us to resent the *real* guys in our lives.

REAL GUYS

Up to this point, we've primarily looked to Edward as an example of what we can seek to find in a guy, but we must now make some distinctions between realism and fantasy. I know it's devastating to come to terms with the following fact, but, the truth is…(brace yourself)…*Edward is not real.* Go ahead; take a moment to grieve if need be.

Even though the *Twilight* superhero is fictional, the good news is that everyday guys *can* be amazing! The problem is that our fantasy-influenced minds often fail to recognize or appreciate those heroes among us—real men, making their mark in a real world. It's not that guys possess *none* of the qualities we adore in men on the big screen; it's that real men have both strengths *and* weaknesses, attractive qualities *and* not-so-glamorous traits, good habits *and* annoying ones. Unlike fictional characters, who are often portrayed as having it *all* together, real people have some things together while other things are…well…an unsightly mess—and that applies to you and me as well!

Although it is not my intention to overly stereotype men—certainly there are considerable differences from one male to the next—I would like to share some of the key ways real men tend to differ from our fantasy-derived superhero, Edward.

Edward Never Has a Bad Hair Day

At first glance, it may seem silly that I brought this up, but it truly is a point worth mentioning. Throughout the *Twilight* storyline, we're told over and over how perfect Edward looks—from his complexion to his hairstyle to his never-aging physique. That makes for great reading, but in real life, no one looks flawless all of the time—and certainly not for *all* of time. As they age, men tend to gain weight in the gut, creating a pregnant-like belly in those lacking a strong commitment to physical fitness. And about half of all men eventually lose their hair. So if the best thing about a man is the way he *looks*, beware. He better have a great personality, too, or you just might be setting yourself up for disappointment in a few years.

Edward Never Wants to Do Anything *More Than He Wants to Be With Bella*

While it's true that when we initially begin seeing a guy, he may lose interest in pretty much everything *except* us, this most certainly will not last. It's not because we somehow lose value over time, but rather, because men tend to thrive on competitive or production-oriented activities. In real life, there would inevitably come a day when Edward would turn to Bella and say, "Instead of watching you sleep all night, do you mind if I go watch the ballgame I recorded earlier today?" Maybe it wouldn't be a ballgame. Maybe he would want to work on a car engine, research how his stock is doing on Wall Street, or try out his new golf clubs. The point is that men, by their very nature, continually seek outlets to experience a sense of accomplishment and victory, and it is often the case that these outlets don't interest or involve us. If we're not careful, we'll take his "outside interests" as a personal rejection and resent him for it.

If you believe your boyfriend or husband is out of balance and invests too much time and energy in outlets that don't involve you, you will want to let a qualified third-party source hear both your side of the story and his. Someone impartial can help identify if one or both of you are out of balance and make practical suggestions.

In summary, don't take it personally and give the man in your life a hard time just because he focuses on other interests sometimes.

Edward Is Smooth With Words

There's a wedding anniversary card my husband gave me some years ago that stands out in my mind. At the bottom of the lovely phrases composed by Hallmark, my husband wrote a single sentence— "Thanks for saying yes." Upon reading that, my eyes instantly dampened with tears. Perhaps you wonder why those four simple words moved me so strongly. It's because Patrick is not one of those guys who effortlessly says things that sweep a girl off of her feet. I guess those men are out there, but my husband is simply not wired in that way. However, it does *not* mean he loves me any less than a man given to poetic eloquence! The simple, yet adorable statement he wrote in that card meant the world to me.

Ladies, most men don't know how to communicate like a cupid-struck "Edward," but that's OK. Appreciate the simple ways that a man expresses affection. Trust me, if you shoot down his imperfect attempts to convey his feelings for you, he'll quit trying.

Edward Is a Mind-Reader

Edward can read others' thoughts, and even though he can't read Bella's mind, it doesn't seem to matter because he's so intuitively in touch with her anyway. In real life, though, it is usually quite the opposite case with men. Oh sure, they know when we're pouting that something is wrong. But other than that, they often seem to overlook things we consider quite obvious.

"He knows I'm having a difficult day; why hasn't he called me?"

"Why would he take me out to a casual restaurant on our anniversary?"

"I showed him the necklace I like; why did he buy me this alarm clock?"

Unlike Edward, real men can't read minds. While we would prefer that they figure out on their own what we like, don't like, and desire from them, it's usually the case that we have to thoroughly explain it—*and sometimes more than once.*

Just this week, I asked a male friend of mine what he was getting his wife for her birthday, and he said, "She told me to get her a card and a dozen roses, so that's what I'm going to get her." He adores his wife, but nonetheless, he needed her to tell him what she wants.

Edward Never Has Financial Pressures

Several men who I spoke with in preparation for writing this book brought up the point that when money is tight, especially within marriage, the stress on a man can become extremely distracting and draining. A woman may resent the fact that her husband is not as spontaneous and fun as he used to be, when the truth is, he is carrying a tremendous burden, and it's taking its toll on him. Of course tight budgets affect women as well, but it is usually the case that men blame the lack of provision primarily on themselves and, as a result, struggle with feelings of inadequacy.

If your man is working hard to make ends meet, be sensitive to how that affects him. He may not be surprising you with exciting date nights or jewelry lately, but don't let this become a source of contention. Rather, affirm and encourage each other through financial challenges.

Edward Never Goes Out With His Buddies

Edward leaves Bella once in a while to go hunting for "nourishment" with his relatives, and also spends one night away from her for his bachelor party. Other than that, he never tells Bella he'd like to go shoot hoops with the guys or watch the Star Wars trilogy at his buddy's house. In actuality, it's beneficial for a man to pal around with his guy friends. I've seen situations where a woman gets jealous and gives her "honey" a hard time when he wants to hang out with his friends. This is a mistake. He should have the liberty to maintain friendships and enjoy his buddies' company, just like we should be free to spend time with our girlfriends on occasion. I realize there are situations when a woman feels her boyfriend or spouse spends too much time with his friends, or hooks up with the *wrong* kind of friends. In such cases, a couple will have to work through those issues. That being said, a man needs to know that he can enjoy male friendships without receiving a guilt trip from the woman in his life.

SHOCKING DISCOVERY: MEN ARE NOT WOMEN

The *Twilight* series was written by a woman, so it makes sense that Edward's character is completely in tune with the female psyche. If you could create a man from scratch, what would he be like? Although I'm sure you and I would differ on a few traits, our lists would probably look a lot alike. Furthermore, I bet both of us would be tempted to make the same mistake—we would likely incorporate *feminine* qualities and tendencies into our man's framework. That's right. As physically attracted as we are to masculinity, we often have a hard time accepting that a man's emotional and psychological makeup are different from ours. Frustration sets in when we fail to understand how men differ from women, and we resent them when, in fact, they are merely behaving like masculine beings.

I once listened to a lady pour out her angry, discontented heart concerning her husband. She couldn't understand why, right when he came home from work, he preferred to relax and watch a ballgame on television for an hour or so rather than take a stroll through the park and talk about his day with her. She wished he was more attentive when she confided in him about her recent struggles with her best friend, and she got frustrated when he surfed the Net on his cell phone at the mall, leaving her to pick out the living room curtains with scarcely any input from him.

I truly empathized with her grief, but the more she spoke, the more I became convinced that she was seriously overlooking something. She complained that she was disappointed that her husband was not acting like more of a *man*, but it seemed to me she was actually disgruntled that he was not behaving more like a *woman*! (Try telling *that* to an already angry lady.)

While I do believe that a man should go out of his way at times to lovingly accommodate his wife's desires, I think we have to be careful not to criticize him simply because he is not "wired" the same way we are. Call me crazy, but I don't know too many men who are eager to walk and talk after a hard day's work, give great advice about "chick" friendship issues, or carry strong opinions about whether a curtain panel looks best in plaid or paisley. There are some things we need our *girlfriends* for!

Did You Know?

Men tend to feel more comfortable talking about emotional topics when we are seated beside them as opposed to across from them. If you sit facing a man and say, "We need to talk," most men will avoid eye contact and squirm in their chair. If you initiate the same conversation while seated beside him on the couch or even in the car, looking straight ahead as opposed to making intense eye contact, he will likely feel more comfortable and therefore open up more during the discussion.

According to Dr. Sax, the author of *Why Gender Matters: What Parents and Teachers Need to Know About the Emerging Science of Sex Differences*, the variances between men and women are not only numerous and significant, but they transcend cultural influences.[2] Men and women are different, *by design*. As we explore these differences, we will see that they are not the result of random evolutionary coincidence, but rather, God's deliberate plan.

BOYS WILL BE BOYS

I found myself observing the children in my daughter's elementary schoolyard one day and couldn't help but chuckle. The girls flocked together on the play equipment and carried on face-to-face conversations while recreating. The boys, on the other hand, played soccer, dodgeball, and tag, and *none* of them engaged in face-to-face conversations for more than a few seconds at a time. Also, whereas the girls were often giggling and some even holding hands, the boys maintained serious expressions as they battled their male classmates in physical competitions—they were obviously *very* determined not to lose.

And there you have it. Guys look for outlets to conquer a challenge and girls look for outlets to connect relationally. That's *not* to say that guys don't enjoy friendships or that girls don't delight in pitching a mean fastball. It's just that when children are given the choice to spend recess doing whatever they want, guys tend to compete while girls primarily converse.

That's fine in elementary school, but how do these gender-driven internal preferences mesh when little boys and girls grow up and commit to lifelong partnerships with one another?

HOW WOMEN SPELL LOVE: *DEVOTION*

A man who understands a woman knows that she desires his *devotion*. Certainly Edward understands this about Bella. We want to be the object of a man's affection, loyalty, attachment, and attention. Furthermore, his devotion is best expressed in the *details*. He acknowledges a recent accomplishment in our lives with a thoughtful card. He cools down the car before we get in on a hot day. He offers to make the kids' lunches for us on mornings when we are clearly running late for an appointment.

The problem is that most men are not so good with relational details and tend to overlook certain subtle, yet important aspects of our lives. This can be infuriating when, for example, he doesn't notice we got a haircut but immediately spots a baseball player's slight decrease in batting average as displayed in tiny text scrolling across the bottom of the television screen.

While men are intrinsically driven to pay attention to the details surrounding their hobbies of interest, a man who wants to please a woman will learn to pay close attention to the details of her life as well.

If a man is not privileged to have had a father-figure in his life model how to treat a woman (or a houseful of outspoken sisters who enlightened him), he likely will have no idea what it is we want or how to go about satisfying our expectations. Then again, he may have a decent grasp of what a woman wants, but over time he has become apathetic and complacent. Either way, the solution is to *lovingly* communicate about the breakdown, and even seek qualified, third-party counsel if need be. There are also a variety of books and curriculum designed to aid couples in this area, and I have listed some excellent materials in the endnotes of this chapter that I highly recommend.[3] The important thing is that we don't resent a man for simply thinking and behaving like a man. It's most often the case that men are not *trying* to sabotage our desire for devotion and emotional intimacy—they just don't understand what in the world we want from them!

> The single greatest tactic women use to seduce married men is to show them an overabundance of respect and admiration. A female comes along and begins esteeming a man as her hero—a true man among boys—and he, in turn, finds her (and her words of affirmation) irresistible, even if, physically speaking, his wife is a much more attractive woman.

HOW MEN SPELL LOVE: *RESPECT*

When Patrick and I were preparing to enter into marriage, I asked him a very important question;

"What do you most want from me as we make a life-time commitment?" His answer was simple yet unforgettable—"Always believe in me."

The same little boys who exert every ounce of energy at recess to win a ballgame eventually grow up to be men who still don't like to lose. In many ways, their manhood is affirmed by their ability to overcome challenges and succeed, thus proving to themselves and others that they are winners, not failures. It is for this reason that men so desperately seek a woman's admiration and respect. We usually don't mean to undermine this need; it just happens naturally. At first, we make fun of him on occasion, then perhaps we begin to criticize some of the decisions he has made, and eventually, if we're not careful, we openly rehearse his failures, our disappointments, and all of the ways he simply does not measure up.

This can produce a lack of confidence in a man that drives him to shrink back from us altogether as he concludes, "I can't live up to her expectations, so I'll just distance myself from her." In his mind, there's no sense in putting his heart and energy into something that he is sure to fail at.

Of course the answer is that he should *not* give up on his helpmate, but rather, work through relational obstacles and challenges with her. *Our* part is to beware of taking criticism too far and destroying the foundation of respect on which men thrive. If you've quit believing in your mate, I assure you, he knows it, and what's more, it is a source of pain and defeat for him. Get counseling, seek healing from past letdowns and mistakes—do whatever it takes to restore mutual respect back to your relationship. This is one area where Bella excels. She continually lets Edward know how much she admires and loves him.

A Lesson I Learned the Hard Way

When feeling a bit neglected or overlooked by our boyfriend or spouse, many of us resort to silent treatments and pouting as a means of enticing him to pay attention to us. We intend that he notice our downcast demeanor and offer us some affection and caring words. Nine times out of ten, however, a man will take our "standoff-ish" attitude as our way of saying, "I'm not pleased with you." Feeling rejected, he will only avoid and ignore us all the more! We then feel appalled that he did not give us the love we desperately wanted, and the next thing you know, World War III breaks out between us!

When you desire affection or attention from your sweetie, simply say, "Honey, I've had a hard day and would like a hug and some attention." That will likely melt his heart and yield the results you're looking for.

SO *WHY* DID GOD DELIBERATELY
CREATE GENDER DIFFERENCES?

All of the struggles we go through to meet the needs of the opposite sex ultimately point us to God; in this way, love and marriage serve as practical teaching tools. After all, God wants the same things from us that men and women want from each other—*respect and devotion.* Just as it takes effort and selflessness for a man and woman to meet each other's gender-specific needs, it takes effort and sacrifice on our part to offer ongoing respect and devotion to God.

Do you live with a healthy fear and respect for God? Do you express devotion to Him in practical, personal ways? More to the point, are you guilty of withholding from God the very things you desire to receive from your mate, such as undivided attention, words of praise and gratitude, and intimacy in the midst of life's distractions and busyness?

As we seek to improve our relationship with the man in our life, or we prayerfully wait for God to bring the right man into our lives, let us be continually aware of *God's* expectations and desires. When we delight ourselves in Him, He gives us the desires of our heart (see Ps. 37:4).

And while we tend to resent gender differences as an ongoing annoyance, they are actually a glorious blessing if we embrace them for what they are—a continual reminder that we must not fixate on what *we* want all of the time, but instead, focus on giving our mate what he needs and giving God what He desires and deserves from us.

A DIRECT ANSWER TO THIS CHAPTER'S QUESTION

Will a man ever love me the way Edward loves Bella? Simply stated, no. Each man loves a woman the best way *he* knows how. He may be an expert on romance or in need of understanding and direction regarding how to express devotion to you, but that's OK. *Real* love requires that two imperfect people work at meeting each other's needs.

And that's the one thing Edward simply is not. *He is not real.*

REFLECTIONS ON ROMANCE—CHAPTER 5

1. In your own words, why is it destructive to cling to a fantasy-based, Hollywood-influenced idea of what men should be like, as opposed to understanding what men are really like?

   _____

   _____

   _____

   _____

2. Look back at each of the points where Edward is contrasted with real men. Is there anything you need to accept about real men?

   _____

   _____

   _____

   _____

3. Did your mom provide a great example, a not-so-great example, or no example at all of how to respect a man? How has this likely affected the way you will (or do) treat a man?

   _____

_____

_____

_____

4. What one thing stands out to you the most when it comes to differences between men and women?

_____

_____

_____

5. (For married readers) Are you guilty of disrespecting your husband, and if so, what are some practical ways you can change that?

_____

_____

_____

6. In what practical ways do you show God devotion? In what practical ways do you show God respect?

_____

_____

_____

_____

_____

PRAYER

Father, You purposed that men and women be different, and in meeting each other's needs, we discover that we must also go beyond our carnal tendencies in order to meet Your desires. Help me to respect You and express devotion to You throughout the day, every day. Father, I also ask that you help me to respect my (future) husband and overcome any bitterness or cynicism that I may be exhibiting. Renew my mind so that I am free to love with a God-kind of love. And show my (future) husband what it means to express devotion, both to you and to me. Help him and me to not only accept each other's differences, but appreciate and enjoy them. In Jesus' name, amen.

Endnotes

1. Stephenie Meyer, *New Moon* (New York: Hachette Book Group USA, 2006), 527.

2. Dr. Leonard Sax, *Why Gender Matters: What Parents and Teachers Need to Know About the Emerging Science of Sex Differences* (New York: Broadway Books, 2005).

3. Recommended reading material:

    A. *For Women Only: What you Need to Know About the Inner Lives of Men*, by Shaunti Feldhahn. NOTE: The companion book for men is *For Men Only: A Straightforward Guide to the Inner Lives of Women*, by Jeff and Shaunti Feldhahn.

    B. *Love & Respect: The Love She Most Desires, The Respect He Desperately Needs*, by Emmerson Eggerichs.

    C. *The Five Love Languages*, by Gary Chapman.

Chapter Six

PURIFIED

How do sex-related decisions heat
up or hinder romance?

*While driving home from work today, my husband
tuned into a radio talk show and listened as the
show's host discussed* Twilight. *The man was
making fun of the fact that Edward doesn't want
to have sex with Bella before marriage and went
on and on about how unrealistic and ridiculous it
is that Stephenie Meyer would create Edward to
be such a "prude and unmanly" character. Prude
and unmanly? If only I could have called in and
spoken up on that radio show! "Mister, don't you
know that it is that very dynamic—Edward's in-
sistence on saving lovemaking for marriage—that
makes the* Twilight *story so steamy and romantic?"*

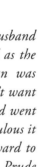

Want to know what else I would have said if I
could have called in? I'd let that guy know
that the word *prude* comes from the word "prudence"

which means *to think before acting*. Isn't thinking before acting an indication of true maturity? And as far as Edward's sexual restraint making him unmanly, well that's just absurd. Any *boy* can give in to hormones and sexual urges but it takes a *real man* to love and respect a woman so much that he insists on controlling himself.

Is it just me or do you find it incredibly chivalrous that Edward wants to wait until he's married to Bella before having sex with her?

SOME THINGS ARE WORTH WAITING FOR

The best way to make your wedding night lame is to have sex beforehand. Just like it's no fun to open a Christmas gift after peeking and knowing exactly what you're unwrapping, there's not a whole lot of excitement in having sex on your wedding night with someone you've already been having sex with. Brides traditionally want their wedding dress to be a surprise for the groom; why not let your beautiful body be a surprise, too?

Truth be told, nothing kindles romance like saving sex for marriage. It keeps things exciting and builds anticipation while dating. Then, even after having been married awhile, an element of excitement about sex remains because, after all, that guy was hard to get. His refusal to have sex with anyone *but* his wife becomes a turn-on when, after marrying him, you're the *one* lucky lady who gets to make love to him. Other women may know him as a friend, co-worker, neighbor, or that handsome man who takes great care of his lawn, but *only you* know him as his lover.

MY STORY

I wish I could say that I waited until marriage to have sex, but unfortunately, that is not the case. It's not fun to admit, but I was a sexually active teen-ager. I hoped that in surrendering my body I would receive the love I so desired, but it only made me more desperate for love.

At 20 years of age, as a sophomore in college, I got engaged to my boyfriend for all the wrong reasons. As previously stated, I thought getting married was the key to happiness; bless my sweet heart and naive mind, right? Our relationship was plagued by conflict and confusion, and I soon started second guessing the engagement. You can imagine how shocked I was when I then discovered that I was pregnant!

I wanted my child to have a mommy *and* a daddy, so I got married, even though our relationship was clearly not healthy. Two years later, he left and married someone else. At just 22 years of age, I was a divorced single mom caring for a precious little girl.

Suddenly, perspective came. God's biblical plan to save sex for marriage made perfect sense, especially when I looked into my daughter's adorable face. She deserved for her parents to love each other and live life together, but, in my rebellion toward God and His standards, she was robbed of that.

These series of events caused me to go humbly to God, repent, and determine to do things *His* way from that point on. Some time later I met Patrick, and early in our relationship we committed to one another to abstain from sex. There was nothing "unmanly" about Patrick as he stood his ground and resisted temptation. On the contrary, I felt more impressed and in love with him as our relationship progressed. His willingness to honor God and respect me by denying himself sexually spoke volumes about his character, maturity, and devotion to Christ and to me.

Patrick and I have now been married for ten years, and I can honestly say that our decision to wait to have sex means as much to me today as it did on our wedding day. There is a trust and mutual respect between us that has remained unshaken over the years.

By God's loving grace, He took the mistakes of my youth and equipped me with a transforming message for parents and young people. I am so passionate about the topic of abstinence and purity that I have written entire books about it and now conduct parent workshops and presentations for teens and young adults. I continue to be amazed at how the Lord took my broken past and turned it into a healing ministry for others.

THE VALUE OF VIRGINITY

There are a variety of modern-day movies that depict men and women trying desperately to lose their virginity. These pathetic films not only infiltrate society with the lie that virginity is a weakness, but their use of off-color humor conveys the notion that sex is trivial, a meaningless act void of all sacredness.

What do you think? *Is losing one's virginity a big deal?* Let's answer this question by first looking at Edward and Bella. Imagine how it would affect the *Twilight* story if, upon meeting Bella, Edward had recently broken up with a girlfriend he'd been having sex with for over a year, and he had a one-night stand with some blonde at a party the week before. Bella had also been sexually active and worried about telling Edward that she has herpes, a sexually transmitted disease that causes her to get blisters "down there."

I have a feeling the *Twilight* series would not have made it to the top sellers list if that's how the story went!

Simply stated, *our virginity is valuable because our future mate is valuable.* Think about it. Had Edward been intimate with other women, even if it was long before meeting Bella, it would have hurt and haunted Bella once she and Edward fell in love. So you see, by valuing his virginity, Edward valued his soul mate, even before he knew her.

Protecting one's virginity lays the ideal foundation for the ultimate romantic experience. After all, there's nothing more romantic than when a man and woman can say to one another, *We are meant for each other in a way that excludes all others and exceeds the intimacy we've experienced with any other.*

Maintaining your virginity is not just about resisting sex until marriage. For starters, it's about honoring God. Second, it's about giving your heart to your husband, even before you meet him. Proverbs 31:12 says that a virtuous woman brings her husband good, not harm, all the days of her life. Did you pick up on the implications of that Scripture? We're to do good to our husbands *all of our lives,* which includes the years *before* we meet him. So you see, when we reserve our heart and body just for him, we are loving him and doing good to him, even though we have yet to meet him. On the contrary, when we give ourselves to other lovers, we are ultimately wounding our husband. We are giving away intimate pieces of our body and soul that belong to him alone.

Simply stated, if you are single, your future mate is worth the wait.

BUT WE'RE IN LOVE!

In all of my discussions with young ladies about sex and dating, most of the girls are convinced that they would not feel comfortable having a casual sexual experience with a stranger or a guy they don't know very well. Their attitude is totally different, however, when it comes to having sex with someone who they love and care for.

There is a prevailing belief today that as long as two people love each other, premarital sex is an acceptable, even beautiful thing. While on the surface this seems reasonable, as we take a closer look and pay attention to God's biblical standards, we realize that such a belief is a serious deception.

First of all, a couple may care for each other very much, only to find that they break up some time later. In such cases, their commitment disappears, but their decision to have sex cannot be undone. The memories, mental images, and emotional ties will remain, and even if they fade somewhat with time, memories and feelings have a way of resurfacing when we least expect it, even after we're married to someone else.

But what about couples like Edward and Bella, who are clearly going to spend the rest of their lives together? They even got engaged—what's wrong with having sex at that point? It comes down to two things:

1. Putting God first

2. Loving versus lusting one another

Putting God First

In my book for parents, *Choosing to Wait,* and my book for teens and singles, *Why Wait?,* I go into great detail about *why* God wants us to reserve sex for marriage. I encourage you to pick up whichever book applies to you so you can fully understand this biblical mandate. For now, let me simply say that God never intended for sex to be experienced apart from marriage. Sex was created to bond two lovers in an exclusive way *after* they commit to each other for life. Now when I say *after they commit to each other for life,* I'm not talking about two high school sweethearts pinky swearing that they are never going to break up. God is looking for a man and a woman to make a covenant commitment through marriage (see Gen. 2:24).

When we ignore God's plan for sex and compromise sexual standards, we are in disobedience to God.

Furthermore, a man and woman living in defiance toward God are setting themselves up for a relationship breakdown. This is why even an engaged couple should wait to have sex. They need to put God first *before* the marriage so that He is first in their lives *after* they say "I do," which is essential if their relationship is going to thrive. You heard my testimony—as a young adult, I violated this principle and paid a *heavy* price.

Loving Versus Lusting One Another

It is often the case that couples have feelings for each other but don't really *love* each other. Oh, they *think* they love each other—they even text "I love you" back and forth several times a day, but in actuality, they *lust* each other. Consider these contrasting attributes:

LOVE	LUST
Desires to satisfy another at the expense of self.	Desires to satisfy self at the expense of another.
Is easily satisfied.	Is never satisfied.
Has nothing to hide.	Often operates in secret.
Brings peace.	Brings guilt.
Is open and honest.	Manipulates and disguises intentions.

LOVE	LUST
Is concerned for another's well being.	Is consumed with selfish desires.
Remains faithful during tough times.	Abandons when needs are not met.
Sees all that is beautiful about a person.	Has eyes fixed primarily on outward beauty.
Is patient.	Is impatient.

When a man can't keep his hands off of us, we tend to feel beautiful, wanted, perhaps even loved, but in reality, we are merely the object of his lust. Think about the way Edward treats Bella. He doesn't want to do *anything* that would cause her to have regret or shame.

When a guy is impatient and doesn't want to wait until marriage to have sex with us, he is violating God's definition of love (see 1 Cor. 13:4). Patience is listed as the very first characteristic of true love. Don't get me wrong, when you develop strong feelings for a man, especially the man you're going to marry, you'll feel anxious to experience physical intimacy with him, but it is your mutual love for one another and Christ that can and should grace you with the patience you need to wait.

In reserving sex for marriage, Edward settles in Bella's heart and mind that she is *loved*, not merely lusted. What's more, he has proven that he has sexual restraint. If a guy can't resist putting the moves on us, what makes us think he'll be able to resist a seductive coworker? In this way, a couple that waits until marriage to have sex creates an uncommon trust and security.

WHAT IF I'VE ALREADY MESSED UP?

If you've had premarital sex, you may be feeling like you've blown it for good and there's nothing you can do now. That is not true. While you cannot erase the past, you can determine to do things differently in the future. It's better to make the decision that, from this day forward, you are going to honor God and reserve your heart and body for your husband rather than concluding, "There's no point in resisting sex now; I've already lost my virginity."

In my book, *Why Wait?* I have an entire chapter that sheds light on picking up the pieces once we decide we no longer want to be sexually active, and I pray you will read it if it applies to you. For now, just know that tomorrow is a new day, and, by God's grace, you can set new standards and expectations for yourself regarding sex.

FOR MARRIED READERS

Did you and your husband have sex before you were married? Perhaps you have been carrying around some shame and regret for not waiting. You may even have resentment toward your husband. Don't cover up those feelings or just settle for living with them; be honest with yourself. If you would like freedom from the guilt of past sexual transgressions, God is ready and willing to forgive. For sexual sins that had nothing to do with your husband, go to God in prayer and release those memories and regrets to Him. For sexual sins involving your husband (if your husband is willing), repent to each other and repent to God together.

SOME FINAL, IMPORTANT SEX-RELATED POINTS

Edward Is Not a Pervert; Your Man Shouldn't Be, Either

While Edward is clearly physically attracted to Bella, he doesn't talk dirty to her or pressure her sexually. He also doesn't make suggestive comments about other women or look at pornography. Whether you are dating or married, don't put up with perversion. If you're dating a guy who seems obsessed with sex, go ahead and end the relationship—trust me, you don't want to try and build a life together with him. If you're married to a man who is somehow sexually out of balance, get counseling and confront those issues.

Perversion always snuffs out the flames of romance because it creates an intimacy barrier between a man and a woman. We want to feel loved by him but instead feel lusted, leaving us unfulfilled and lonely.

Only Edward Could Sleep in Bella's Bed With Her and Resist Having Sex

The reason Edward could handle being in bed with Bella before they were married without having sex with her is because he's a make-believe character! A guy who is really attracted to a girl will find it nearly impossible to snuggle up in bed with her at night without experiencing strong sexual temptation. If you are going to resist having premarital sex, you and your sweetheart are going to have to set some practical boundaries. You will want to avoid too much alone time in settings where physical activity could easily take place. (This most certainly includes the bed!) Setting these kind of boundaries does not just apply to young teens; grown-ups who are dating need to avoid situations where they become sexually vulnerable as well.

There's a Reason Edward, Bella, and Jacob Are All Inexperienced

Stephenie Meyer purposely includes text in the *Twilight* series that lets readers know that Edward, Bella, and Jacob are all inexperienced at sex and love.

She does this on purpose to make the story more spicy and exciting because Stephenie knows what I want to make sure you know as well—*there's nothing romantic about having a slew of past lovers.*

Beware of modern dating trends that encourage singles to go from one good-looking guy to the next, playing the field while giving away priceless pieces of our body and soul. We don't find our mate by kissing one "frog" after another until we find our prince. We save our kisses until our prince finds us! (More about how to find a mate in an upcoming chapter.)

Edward Doesn't Surround Himself With Sexually Graphic Media

We never read about Edward blaring sexually explicit rap songs while driving through Forks or setting his DVR to record a sitcom full of perverted scenes and innuendoes. Stephenie created Edward as a classy character, and classy people don't enjoy trashy entertainment. On a practical note, the more we set our eyes on sexually graphic images, the more our sexual appetite is stirred, thus undermining our intentions to remain abstinent before marriage. Even after marriage, we don't want to compromise our relationship with Christ by exposing our eyes and ears to images and words that mock what God stands for. There's no television show, song, or Website that's worth grieving God and inciting perversion in our heart.

> "Adolescents who watch television with high levels of sexual content are twice as likely to initiate sexual intercourse and also more likely to initiate other sexual activities."[2]

WHAT ABOUT JACOB?

We've just looked at Edward and Bella as an example of how loving one person for a lifetime is the ultimate romantic experience, but what about Jacob? Doesn't Bella love him, too? We'll not only explore Jacob's role in Bella's life in the next chapter; we'll also look at how "Jacob" just might come along in your life as well.

REFLECTIONS ON ROMANCE—CHAPTER 6

1. Have you ever "fooled around" with a guy in hopes of feeling loved? If so, describe how you felt in the end. If not, write down why that doesn't work.

_____

_____

_____

_____

_____

_____

2. In your own words, why is virginity valuable?

_____

_____

_____

_____

_____

_____

3. How does it affect a couple to know they have each had previous lovers?

_____

_____

_____

_____

_____

_____

4. Take a look at the differences between love and lust. Which one stands out the most to you, and why?

_____

_____

_____

_____

_____

5. (For single readers) If you have already had premarital sex and have never repented for it, write down your prayer of repentance and ask the Lord to restore your standards of purity.

    (For married readers) If you and your husband had sex before marriage, write him a letter asking forgiveness for that and explain how you want to uphold God's standards for purity, even as it relates to media choices.

_____

_____

_____

_____

_____

_____

PRAYER

Lord, we know our spiritual enemy seeks to exploit our sexual innocence as early in our lives as possible. We also know that You intend for sex to be a beautiful, blessed act, which is why you have given us boundaries and standards. Please heal me of sexual sins committed against me and forgive me for my sexual sins—those I have acted on as well as those that have taken place in my mind and heart. Help me to honor You in what I choose to watch on television and listen to on the radio. Guard my eyes and ears from words and images that grieve Your righteous standards, and pour out blessings on the physical intimacy between me and my (future) husband. In Jesus' name, amen.

Endnotes

1. Stephenie Meyer, *Breaking Dawn* (New York: Hachette Book Group USA, 2008), 25.
2. http://www.puremorality.org/NCCPCFstats.htm.

Chapter Seven

ADDICTED

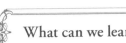

What can we learn from Jacob?

While watching New Moon *on the big screen, the lady sitting next to me nearly choked on her Coke when Jacob Black took off his shirt. The predominately female theater audience went insane at the sight of the part-man, part-werewolf's washboard abs and massive "guns." (My family calls biceps "guns" for some reason.)*

*T*wilight fans everywhere are torn. There's Edward, with his sparkling white skin, polished wardrobe, and gentle personality. Then there's Jacob—tan, aggressive, and not afraid to get dirty (oh, and he happens to have the *perfect* physique, too). Those of us living vicariously through Bella are divided. Which man should I choose? More to the point, which T-shirt do I buy—*Team Edward* or *Team Jacob*?

Twilight fans aren't the only ones confused. Bella struggles with an internal tug-o-war as well. She obviously clings to her first love, Edward, yet finds it impossible to let go of her gorgeous, loyal heartthrob, Jacob. They both love her. They both fight for her. And they *both* have a place in her heart.

DO YOU HAVE A "JACOB" IN YOUR LIFE?

It's not likely that you have formed a meaningful relationship with Taylor Lautner, the actor who plays the part of Jacob Black in the *Twilight* movies, but you just might have a "Jacob" in your life. Allow me to explain.

"Jacob" is that guy who you are drawn to primarily because you find him breathtakingly handsome. You like being around him, but there's something about him that disqualifies him from being your "Edward"—the man you want to spend the rest of your life with. You know you will never marry "Jacob," but you struggle with letting him go. For reasons you may or may not understand, you are reluctant to "toss him back into the sea."

Then again, "Jacob" could be that guy that, at one time, you honestly believed you could be with forever, but soon realized that he's not good for you. Perhaps he gets angry easily and turns into a "werewolf," mistreating you in a way that you know is unacceptable. Maybe he lacks the spiritual maturity and commitment to Christlike living that you do. No matter the case, you know you don't belong with him. The problem is that you feel like you can't cut him out of your life—like you *need* him.

"Jacobs" are those guys who are always there when our "Edward" hurts our feelings or leaves us. He's the one we can run to, even if weeks or months have passed since we last spoke to him. He cares about us, accepts us, and, in many ways, seems to know us better than almost anyone else. It's also obvious he finds us attractive.

Even though, deep down, we know we don't want a long-term romantic relationship with him, a miserable jealousy rises up inside our soul when we think about him falling in love with someone else. We don't want him, but we don't want him to move on and find someone else, either.

WHAT'S WRONG WITH HOLDING ON TO "JACOB"?

It may seem innocent enough that "Jacob" is continually there behind the scenes taking our occasional late-night phone calls and sending us texts from time to time—"How are you? I miss talking to you. Hope to see you soon." In actuality, there are some real repercussions that can occur as a result of holding on to "Jacob." Consider the following:

"Jacob" Creates Intense Physical Temptation

As previously mentioned, we usually find "Jacob" extremely attractive; as a matter of fact, that is likely a driving factor in our decision to keep him in our lives. He smells good, has a laugh that creates butterflies in our stomach, and perhaps has a smile that takes our breath away. What's more, "Jacob" knows we get weak in the knees around him. In an effort to take our relationship with him to the next level, he will likely turn up the heat through seduction. If he can't get us to give into him *emotionally*, perhaps we will give in *physically*.

Just like Jacob Black tried to win Bella's heart with a spontaneous, passionate kiss, the "Jacob" in our lives will likely create physical temptation. Oh sure, we're tempted with "Edward," too, but there's a difference. "Edward" focuses on winning our heart; "Jacob" usually goes after our body.

We've already discussed the reasons that premarital physical activity is not God's will for our lives. It is for this reason that we need to beware of "Jacob." Even though we experience an invigorating rush when he's around, his presence opens an unnecessary door to physical temptation.

It is also selfish of us to keep "Jacob" hanging on.

"Jacob" Needs to Move On

Our back-and-forth, "I was into you yesterday but not as much today," behavior tends to create an obsessive response from "Jacob." We become a challenge, and this incites heightened pursuit from him. We may find ourselves enjoying the control and attention this dynamic creates, but truth be told, we're just being selfish. We know we're not going to make a lasting commitment to him, so we should end things so he can move on. However, just telling "Jacob" to move on won't do the trick—didn't Bella try that? We have to stop toying with his emotions and end communication.

We make a real mess of things when we try to keep the relationship going by saying, "We're just friends." *Friends* don't struggle to avoid making out. Furthermore, it's one thing to have always been just friends with a guy; it's another thing to try and become "just friends" after having been more than friends in the past. It's nearly impossible to keep boundary lines from blurring when we spend time with a guy we've previously dated.

My husband once explained to me that if you really want a guy to move on, you have to cut off communication because, as long as you're willing to give him time and attention, even if it's minimal, he will likely believe that he still has a chance.

Obviously if "Jacob" is abusive, there becomes a heightened need to end the relationship. In short, if you know you're not going to marry a guy, don't use him as a stand-in until "Edward" comes along. Let him go so he can move on. And whatever you do, don't go running back to him *after* you've let him go.

"Jacob" Isn't the Person to Run to When We're Down

Bella began spending lots of time with Jacob when Edward left, and as a result, Jacob fell for her. Then Edward returned and Bella no longer needed to spend all that time with Jacob. She basically dropped him like a rotten potato. *That's no way to treat someone.*

When we feel lonely, depressed, or unlucky at love, that's when we're the most tempted to reach out to "Jacob." Knowing we have a special place in his heart makes it all the more tempting because we know he will respond favorably to us. When we begin spending time with him again, he offers his shoulder to cry on and cheers us up, and it feels good. The problem with this scenario is that we are using "Jacob;" we are taking advantage of his feelings for us.

We are also creating a situation that could be lethal later down the line when we're married.

"Jacob" Will Haunt You Later in Life

Even if you marry the most romantic, handsome, thoughtful, talented, honest, loyal, fun, caring man in the world like I did, there will be seasons when your feelings for him seem numb. Whether it's due to conflict, disappointment because he somehow let you down, or just the emotional doldrums that can set in at times as a couple lives everyday life together, at some point you will wonder where the goose bumps and giggles went. *And this is when "Jacob" haunts us.*

We remember how much "Jacob" cared about us, how he was always there for us, how gorgeous he was, and how special he made us feel. Ironically, we don't recall all the things we *didn't* particularly like about him; we only remember the best of times.

When we were young and our love life was challenged, we ran to "Jacob." Now we're married, and guess who we're dying to run to? You guessed it. We long to be with "Jacob" once again.

Social technology has lots of benefits, but also creates some new challenges. Whereas in decades past it was fairly difficult to find someone you hadn't talked to in years, now it can take just a few *seconds* to reunite with an old flame. Email, Facebook, Skype—I'm sure there will be new technology even before this book hits the stores, but you understand what I'm saying. It's easy to find "Jacob" again, and when we do, we not only betray our spouse, but we bust the door wide open for an extramarital affair. What's more, we are deceived. We are *seriously* taking our spouse for granted while also majorly making "Jacob" out to be a hero that he simply is not. We didn't want to be with "Jacob" when we had the chance; if we pursue him later in life, we'll end up realizing once again why we are *not* meant to be with him.

Please don't misunderstand me—when we're married, we don't get the luxury of reuniting with a past flame to see if there's still some chemistry there. Marriage is a commitment to *forsake all others*, and that includes "Jacob." And when our feelings for our spouse are at an all-time low, that's when we need to invest more time and energy into our relationship with *him* as opposed to seeking out "Jacob." We don't want our husbands looking for love elsewhere when his feelings for us are taking a downward nosedive, do we?

There's nothing pleasant about being married and having feelings for someone other than our spouse, which is why maintaining wise boundaries when we're single is so beneficial. You won't *always* be single, you know, and the emotional ties you make today can become a frustrating knot later. This is why, girlfriend, you must end it with "Jacob." Until you do, you're not ready to meet the love of your life, which happens to be the subject of our next chapter.

Married readers, even though you're past the point of meeting "Edward," I have truths in the next chapter especially for you, including a section entitled, "Help, I Married the Wrong Man!"

REFLECTIONS ON ROMANCE—CHAPTER 7

1. Do you have a "Jacob" in your life? If so, why do you find it so hard to let go?

   _____

   _____

   _____

   _____

   _____

2. (For married readers) What would you want your husband to do if he had a woman from his past that he feels emotionally tied to? Are you willing to take your own advice?

   (For single readers) What would you say to your future spouse right now if he is currently forming strong emotional bonds with another girl? Are you willing to take your own advice?

   _____

   _____

   _____

   _____

   _____

3. If you have a "Jacob" in your life, what
   are some practical things you need to do
   to end the relationship?

_____

_____

_____

_____

4. Write down why it's important to you to
   avoid keeping "Jacob" hanging on.

_____

_____

_____

_____

PRAYER

*Lord, I know that you intend that a man
and woman reserve their hearts and bodies
exclusively for each other. Please help me to
honor Your standards and "forsake all others."
Give me the wisdom to avoid the "Jacobs" in
life as I strive to honor the man you do have
for me. Teach me how to guard my heart so
that I do not form intimate bonds with men
who are not my spouse. Last but not least,*

Lord, help me to invest my time, energy, and attention into my (future) husband and not take him for granted.

Endnote

1. Stephenie Meyer, *Eclipse* (New York: Hachette Book Group USA, 2007), 525.

Chapter Eight

FOUND

 How do I find my "Edward"?

I'm sure you remember the story of how Bella and Edward met. Bella's out-of-state friend Maria calls her up and tells her about a great guy named Edward who goes to her school. Bella's heart leaps, and she thinks, "Surely he's the one for me!" Out of sheer determination to meet him, she packs up and moves to Maria's hometown, Forks, Washington. Bella sneaks into the school counselor's office and pulls up Edward's schedule, then makes up an excuse to convince the counselor to put her in one of Edward's classes—his biology class. Desperate to talk to him at school the next day, Bella can't sleep; she's too preoccupied conjuring up one strategy after another, plotting how to strike up a conversation with him.

Dressed in the most figure-hugging outfit she owns, Bella gets to school early the next day, asks around until she finds out who Edward's lab partner is, then pays the girl to request a new partner. When Bella finally walks into biology and spots the picturesque Edward, she is delighted to sit down in the empty chair next to him. Determined to get his attention, she purposely leans way over while staring into the microscope on their table, knowing Edward has a great view of her cleavage. "That's sure to get him interested," she thinks to herself.

LADY, WHAT BOOK DID YOU READ?

You and I both know that is not at all how Edward and Bella met. In quite the opposite fashion, their paths effortlessly crossed on a seemingly ordinary day without any premeditated planning whatsoever. Her schedule happened to put her in the same class with Edward, and he was conveniently in need of a lab partner. Bella did not play the part of a seductress and flaunt her body to get his attention; she was simply herself. And guess what? It worked! Edward was intensely drawn to her—*and the rest is history.*

YOUR PLIGHT TO MEET MR. RIGHT

There are two ways you can approach the issue of trying to find your future mate. You can rely on God and have faith or rely on yourself and have anxiety.

Consider this biblical promise, *"Trust in the Lord with all of your heart, and lean not on your own understanding; In all of your ways acknowledge Him and He shall direct your paths"* (Prov. 3:5-7 NKJV). Did you catch that? When we trust God, as opposed to our limited ability to control everything, He will direct our paths, meaning He will orchestrate where our life takes us and who we meet. That's right; the same God who put countless stars in their place, tilted the earth on its precise axis, and knows exactly how many particles of dust are hovering just above your head at this very instant is willing and ready to direct your path so that, at just the right moment in time, your life collides with a man whom you would delight in marrying.

The alternative to trusting God to bring your mate into your life is to rely on yourself and frantically search for "the one." Most young ladies who go this route try everything from joining multiple church singles groups to frequenting the town dance hall in hopes that the man of their dreams will notice them in their tight jeans and ask them to two-step. (At least, that's how it works in Texas.)

When women believe it's all up to them to find and procure a mate, they live with the nagging feeling that they may or may not run into the right guy depending on the hand fate deals them. This reliance on happenstance can cause a woman to become frantic; she's under the gun to snag a great guy before some other gal beats her to him!

As I'm sure you've already concluded, it's much less stressful to simply trust God and look to Him to bring all of the important pieces of our life's love story together. There are numerous Scriptures that assure us that our lives are not the end result of random events, but rather, are orchestrated by God, especially when we are seeking to know and follow His will. That being said, there's no need to worry that we'll somehow fail to cross paths with "Edward" or that some lucky woman will win his heart before we have even had a chance to meet him. With God calling the shots, our destiny will unfold daily; no need to worry.

The only word of caution I want to add is that if you are an antisocial person who avoids friendly conversations with the opposite sex, then you are not doing your part to meet your special someone. When God does His part and brings "Edward" across our path, our part is to be willing to respond. We can hinder God's plan by avoiding "Edward," or worse, running him off with a stuck-up attitude. Trusting God to bring us a mate means we avoid anxiously looking for a spouse, but we *do* keep an open mind, a willing heart, and a watchful eye. Perhaps that attractive, friendly guy we keep running into at

Starbucks would make a great hubby. You'll never know if you keep avoiding him!

THE WRONG WAYS TO TRY
TO FIND YOUR MATE

Here are some common ways young ladies (and older women) try to get a man, along with an explanation of why it's not wise.

Relying on Seduction

As previously mentioned, it wasn't Bella's bosom that caught Edward's attention. When we use our seduction and sexuality to attract a man, we become a magnet for lustful men while *repelling* godly men, the very ones who have marriage potential. A good guy (a.k.a. a *godly* guy), looks for a girl with class, and there's nothing classy about—as my father-in-law would say—a woman with ten pounds of potatoes shoved into a five-pound sack! (That's his way of describing a female whose clothes are too tight.)

I like how Chad Eastham puts it: *Do you dress like a target or a treasure?*[2] If your wardrobe accentuates your breasts and bottom, you're going to attract guys who are only after your breasts and bottom, thus you become the *target* of their lustful, perverse intentions. By contrast, while a godly man will most certainly appreciate your outward beauty, he'll also value your modesty and *treasure* you for much more than your figure (which is good because after you have babies, our figures tend to...well...reconfigure!).

In short, don't use your body as bait to catch a man. You are not some slimy, cheap earthworm; you're an intriguing, godly woman with a smart brain and vibrant personality—that's the "hook" your future mate will fall in love with.

Hanging out at Funky Fred's Freaky Night Club

In my opinion, nightclubs are not where singles should go to meet a man. I am aware that there are those who would disagree with me. They want to know, "What's wrong with a casual setting that involves upbeat music, social drinking, and some flirtation with the opposite sex?" The problem with nightclubs is that they tend to draw a crowd of people who are looking for a quick hook-up experience. Men arrive alone but hope to leave with a companion for the night. Not only that, nightclubs are usually absurdly smoky, full of drunk people who *think* they can dance, and the music lyrics are a far cry from God-honoring.

Put it this way; if making a love match is about finding the right fish in the sea, nightclubs are where bottom feeders hang out. Knowing this, many singles go to church to find a man.

Going to Church Just *to Find a Husband*

As Christians, it's essential that we have a church family—not just a building we go to on Sundays but a group of fellow Christ followers who know us, care about us, and inspire and motivate us in our walk with the Lord. Having said that, it's quite a different thing to attend or join a church for the *sole purpose* of hoping to meet a man there. While I encourage singles to involve themselves in singles ministry, we need to be careful. Sometimes Christian singles groups are actually just the nightclub "bottom feeders" dressed in their Sunday best. In other words, the group is more focused on romantic opportunities than on serving God alongside their unmarried brothers and sisters in Christ.

While I *do* believe a single woman should be on the watch for a potential love match within her church community, don't cheapen your church experience by making it *all* about that. Focus on worshiping and serving the Lord with your church family, and if your future husband happens to be a member there, God will make sure you two spot each other and hit it off.

Chasing After a Married Man

I don't know that too many women say to themselves, "I want to fall in love with a married man." I think what happens more often is that a woman wants to find someone who would make a great family man, and, as a result, finds herself attracted to a man with a wife and family. No matter the case, there is *never*—under any circumstance—*ever,* a viable reason to pursue a romantic relationship with a married man. I don't care if he's on the verge of divorce, married to the world's meanest woman, or says he's attracted to you far more than he has *ever* been to his wife; stay far, far away from him!

A man either respects the sacredness of marriage or he doesn't. Furthermore, if he will cheat *with* you, he'll cheat *on* you.

One more thing: A man whose wife is dying is *not* available. He might be a great man and a wonderful father, and it might be easy to picture yourself comforting him in his time of sorrow—and filling the void when his wife is gone. Don't fall into that trap. Bring a casserole, but don't be the shoulder he cries on. He doesn't need temptation on top of everything else, and you don't want to be the rebound wife.

Entering into a romantic relationship with a married man is what the Bible calls the sin of *adultery*, and the Lord does not tolerate it. In my opinion, being the "other woman" in a married man's life is one of the single most selfish acts a woman can commit. How would you feel if a sweet-talking lady came along and seduced the father of your children? Even if *he's* the one who initiates the affair, as females, we need to have each other's back. You don't have to know a man's wife in order to say to yourself, "That man is off limits. There is a woman out there who has entrusted her heart to him and committed to love him for the rest of her life."

There will *never, ever* be a time when it's God's will for you to be with someone else's husband, so don't even consider it! And while we're on the topic, please resist the urge to flirt, flaunt your body, or form emotional ties with a married man. As author and Bible teacher Beth Moore once put it, *that's something only mean girls do.*

LORD OF THE RING

I know this is a *Twilight*-themed book, but I want to share a story with you that involves the Lord and a special ring.

After my divorce, I wondered if I would ever meet a godly man and experience a healthy marriage. My sister had recently given me a sterling silver ring with a cross on it, and as I was praying one day about my love-related hopes and fears, I felt led by the Lord to put that ring on my ring finger where a wedding band normally goes. In that moment, the Lord spoke to my heart and assured me that He would be like a husband to me while I was single. He also impressed the following promise on my soul:

"When the timing is right, and the man *I* have set apart for you comes along, I will confirm that it's time to take off this ring and accept a ring from him."

I felt so very comforted by this experience, and I wore the ring everyday as reminder of God's special promise to me.

Even though I was single and desired a husband, I did not participate in the traditional dating scene. Just as He had promised, I trusted God to show me who my husband was without having to try out one guy after another. Eventually, a friend of mine began going on and on about this guy she knew and what a great couple we would make. She described him as having an uncommon passion for the Lord and an outgoing, awesome personality. The problem was, he lived over 200 miles away from me. When he moved to my same city a couple of months later, however, I figured I should at least meet him.

We visited at church on a couple of occasions, then eventually went out to dinner. I had an amazing time with him. I came home from our evening together and prayed; "Lord, this guy seems to really love You, and I could see myself with someone like him. Please confirm your will in my life; I don't want to keep spending time with him if he's not the one."

I said "amen," then noticed something about my silver cross ring. *The band was broken in half.* In that moment, I felt the Lord was fulfilling His promise—this guy had the Lord's blessing to be in my life.

As time went on and I got to know him better, I became increasingly convinced that he and I were meant to be together for the rest of our lives. The day came when he gave me a beautiful engagement ring, and I recalled how God had promised that day would come.

This is the story of how I came to realize that Patrick was the one for me.

I did not tell you that testimony so that you would seek some mystical sign as proof that you're supposed to marry a certain someone, and I certainly don't advise that you run out and buy a cross ring in hopes that the band will break when you meet your future mate! I shared that story to assure you that, in His own ingenious way, God will confirm His will when you've met the right man. There's no telling just how He'll do it, but one thing is for sure—if you are seeking His blessing, God will make His will known to you in a personal, unmistakable way.

Now let's address a concern women commonly express: "I think I married the wrong man!" Whether you're looking for a mate or already married, there is a lesson to be learned here.

HELP! I MARRIED THE WRONG MAN!

When my husband comes home from work, I may not get as giddy as Bella does when she sees Edward, but I honestly do feel excited to see him. He is my best friend, and I adore him. Having said that, we have gone through marital challenges and experienced seasons in the past when we were *not* so thrilled to see each other. We've even had moments in our relationship that were so low that I sincerely wondered, "Did I marry the wrong guy, Lord?" Yep, even after that dramatic ring experience and all the confirmation I received while we were dating and engaged, I wondered if I misunderstood God's leading. I don't entertain that thought for very long, however, because I know that's an age-old tactic of our spiritual enemy. If he can convince us we married the wrong man, he can tempt us to look for a new one, thus destroying our family, which is his ultimate goal for my household and yours.

As we prayerfully seek out a mate, let us not fall into the trap of thinking there's a guy out there who is *perfect* for us. No matter who you marry, he's going to frustrate you at times, and you are going to get on his last nerve on occasion. It's easy during these times to wonder if we missed God's leading and married the wrong person, but the truth is, if you married someone else, he would have other irritating issues, and you would get just as annoyed with him as you do with your hubby now.

I've heard some people argue against the notion that God has a mate picked out for us. All I know is that if we pray about who we should marry, the Lord will lead us. In addition, He gives us instructions in His Word, many of which we have addressed in this book, about what kind of qualities we should look for in a mate. Some people follow these instructions and are shocked when their marriage is still trying and hard at times. Other people don't follow the instructions and then, when their marriage is suffering, wonder if they should get a divorce and try again doing things God's way. No matter the case, the answer is *not* to get a divorce and look for a new man, but rather, trust that God knew exactly who you were going to marry and has planned your life accordingly. In other words, you're not forever out of God's will because of who you married.

I recently heard the story of a young married woman who made a list of everything she *wished* her husband would be—more committed to physical fitness, more social, more educated…the list went on and on. Her conclusion: "I want a divorce. I married the wrong man."

My three-part response to her:

A new man just means a new list.

Why would your husband strive to be a better man for you when you're sitting around making long lists of his shortcomings?

Funny how you're failing to see *your own* shortcomings.

You've heard the cliché, *bloom where you are planted.* That's my advice to those who fear they committed their lives to the wrong man. God will grace you to love him—that man you married, for better or worse—and in the process, you will become more Christlike. Furthermore, studies indicate that couples who report being unhappy in their marriage but who stayed together report being happy with their relationship when asked again years later.

There are times when, due to abuse or infidelity, two people may need to separate and seek counseling. For most of us, however, we will encounter trying circumstances that naturally occur when two lives attempt to blend into one. In such cases, we should cling to our spouse and fight for our marriage. We vowed to do so; now let us keep our marital commitment.

THE BEST APPROACH TO
FINDING A LOVE MATCH

In case you haven't noticed, I like to list information as bold points so they are organized and easily understood. When it comes to the best way to find a love match, however, I don't have any such list. I have one simple, yet powerful, piece of advice. If you want to meet a godly mate, focus on your relationship with Christ, and everything will fall into place in time. If you have cultivated a tender heart toward the Holy Spirit and a keen knowledge of God's Word (the Bible), you'll meet the *right* guy at the *right* time, and you'll be confident that marrying him is the *right* decision.

It's not uncommon for women to wonder, What if it's not God's will that I get married? First of all, it's highly unlikely that He wants you to remain single all of your life because God delights in marriage and children. If, for some reason, He has plans for you that do not involve marriage, there will be a grace on your life to remain single, and God will satisfy your soul.

If you are single, and perhaps several years or more past the age at which you hoped to be married, that last sentence may have seemed irritatingly trite – *"… there will be a grace on your life to remain single, and God will satisfy your soul."* I get it. It's annoying for a lady who has been married for a decade and has four children to make such a casual statement. As if it's that easy!

If that's what you're thinking and feeling, allow me to share a few things from my heart to yours.

I don't claim to know why you aren't married yet or what God's up to in your life specifically, but I do know this—I wanted to have a family more than anything in the whole world, and now that I do, I *still* have to rely on God's grace and allow Him to satisfy my soul! You need God's grace to be single, and I need God's grace to be a wife and mother; in that sense, we're both in the same boat. My side of the boat has some dirty diapers floating around and perhaps yours has some frozen dinners—reminiscent of occasional lonely nights—but we *both* must look to God to help us navigate through the choppy waters of daily life.

Remember the "munchies of the soul" illustration from the first chapter? Well, getting married doesn't indefinitely cure our internal munchies. No matter the season of life, unless we seek out a meaningful, daily connection with God, we will just end up making the same ole' rounds in the all too familiar "kitchen" of inner dissatisfaction.

Allow me to reiterate that it is *not* likely that God is calling you to be single all of your life. The fact that you long to get married is a good indication that the Lord is preparing your heart to meet your future mate. It may take longer than you would like, but I've watched as, time and time again, God faithfully honors a woman's prayer and blesses her with a godly mate.

If you are a "more seasoned" woman now single after past failed relationships and you hope to find true love, take your desire to God in prayer. If *anyone* can add a new chapter to your life's love story, it's Him.

Whatever you do, don't lose heart and marry the wrong person just because you're anxious to experience married life. Enjoy your time as a single woman. Go on mission trips, enjoy getaways with your girlfriends, and cover your bedroom in feminine décor. Before you know it, you'll most likely be married and reminiscing on all the fun you had before you tied the knot.

Some of the best times I ever experienced in the Lord's presence occurred when I was single—worshiping Him by myself yet sensing I was far from alone.

REFLECTIONS ON ROMANCE—CHAPTER 8

1. Meditate on Proverbs 3:6-7: *"Trust in the Lord with all of your heart and lean not on your own understanding; in all of your ways acknowledge Him, and He shall direct your paths."* Write down the ways you currently are or are not living by the instructions in this passage.

   _____

   _____

   _____

   _____

   _____

2. When you encounter an attractive guy, do you come on overly strong? Do you avoid him at all costs? How might you need to change and improve your interaction with men?

   _____

   _____

   _____

   _____

   _____

3. Look back at the wrong ways to meet a man described in this chapter. Which one speaks to you the most, and why?

_____

_____

_____

_____

4. Are you part of a loving, spiritually healthy church family? If not, what can you do this week to make strides toward getting involved?

_____

_____

_____

_____

5. (Single readers) Write out a prayer to God expressing your trust in Him to cross your path with the man you're going to marry.

(Married readers) Write out a prayer to God expressing your trust in Him to breathe new life into Your marriage.

_____

_____

_____

_____

_____

_____

_____

_____

_____

PRAYER

Father, we often live as if You are a million miles away and unaware of our everyday experiences and interactions. On the contrary, You are actively working in the midst of our daily decisions, friendships, and relationships. Renew my mind so that my heart can trust that You truly are in control, and therefore, I have nothing to be anxious about or fear. I entrust my life to You, and rest in the knowledge that You care about my love-related desires and are well able to put the finishing touches on my love story. Satisfy my soul with Your love.

Endnotes

1. Stephenie Meyer, *Twilight* (New York: Hachette Book Group USA, 2005), 43.
2. See Chad Eastham, *Guys Like Girls Who...* (Nashville: Thomas Nelson, 2008).

Chapter Nine

COMMITTED

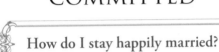

How do I stay happily married?

*Edward and Bella's wedding was magical. And their honeymoon...a private island? Does it **get** any more romantic than that? Edward and his bride spend a blissful month lying side-by-side on the shoreline, making love whenever the mood strikes them and falling asleep in each other's arms. It's practically heaven on earth—until Bella becomes hellaciously sick! The newlyweds return home to face a myriad of unforeseen obstacles.*

Sorry, Ed and Bell; the honeymoon is over.

WHERE DID THAT HAPPY COUPLE GO?

Like *Twilight's* leading lovers, most couples are on top of the world at their wedding and spend their honeymoon intoxicated by their mutual love and attraction. They exchange kisses every chance they get and call each other names like *cutie patootie, sweetie pie,* and *boo bear.* The days and weeks following the wedding can seem too good to be true. Unfortunately, for every married couple I've ever known, that euphoric state *is* too good to be true—at least for very long.

When the honeymoon is over and a man and woman begin living everyday life together, it's not uncommon for them to become sick—sick of each other! Suddenly the way he repeatedly clears his throat at 5:00 A.M. every morning makes her want to scream; "Doesn't he care that I'm trying to sleep?" He feels like he's going to go "ape" if she tells him one more time to hang that picture in the entryway; "Doesn't she have something better to do than nag me about a stupid picture?"

The personality quirks we once found adorable in our mate often become the grounds for nuclear war after we've been married awhile. I recall a giggly bride-to-be commenting at her bridal shower, "Jeff always wipes his wet hands on the decorative towel in my parent's guest bathroom even though I've told him that's what the less formal hand towel is there for; he's so silly!" I thought to myself, "Girl, this time next year you're gonna want to *kill* him when he does that in your bathroom."

While some couples experience greater marital conflict than others, nearly every married person will agree that there are some real ups and downs. It's important to note that behind the petty annoyances usually lie deep wounds. Perhaps she believes he no longer takes the time to really listen to her. He may feel like she's always telling him what to do, as if he's not man enough to think for himself. Deep-down hurts can manifest in seemingly silly ways, like engaging in an all-out standoff over who gets to put their bagel in the toaster first, for example.

There are numerous books and resources available that do an excellent job addressing the intricacies of marriage and providing solutions to specific challenges, and I've provided some suggested materials in the endnotes in Chapter Three. What I would now like to do is share my Six Cs. They provide a big-picture strategy for maintaining love over the long haul.

1. *Stay* Connected.

There's a downward progression that tends to plague married couples. They start out as best friends and passionate lovers, only to look up some years later and realize that they've become little more than roommates, strangers living under the same roof. This distance did not settle in overnight; it is the end result of neglecting each other and taking each other for granted, day after day.

One of the best words of advice I can offer any married couple is to *put your marriage first.* If it means little Johnny has to participate in one extra-curricular activity instead of three so that you and your spouse have time together, so be it. I've seen couples get so busy with their kids, careers, and even ministry activities that their marriage falls apart. That's crazy! It's far more beneficial to have your marriage intact than to be promoted at work, for example. Take a look at what time commitments are hindering your marriage and, if at all possible, cut back.

My husband and I send the kids to their rooms around 9:00 P.M. on weeknights so that we can talk and catch up about the day's events. While the kids occasionally sigh in disappointment when we announce it's time for Mom and Dad to have their time together, I also get the idea that they experience a security of sorts knowing that we enjoy being together. There's nothing wrong with asking the kids to give you and your spouse some time alone.

In the midst of your busy schedule, make sure you plan date nights. I also suggest that a married couple get away for at least a day or two together every few months. With our family dynamics, that's hard for us to do, but maintaining a love connection with my husband is worth the effort.

As we manage the household with our spouse, we may fall in to the "efficiency" trap, which is where everything we do centers around productivity. Our once loving and often playful communication is reduced to a robotic checklist:

"Did you check the mail?"

"Yes. Did you get groceries for tonight?"

"Not yet. Are we going to the PTA meeting at 7:00 P.M.?

"You go to the meeting; I'll take Amy to ballet. Before we go to bed, we need to sign the tax papers."

There's no way around the duties that go hand-in-hand with running a household together, but don't let that be *all* you and your hubby do! We need to have *fun* with our spouse, too. Who says the two of you can't go to the water park without the kids once in a while? Whatever hobbies or forms of recreation you and your husband enjoy, make time for it. Or go discover some new interests together!

If you're married, when was the last time you had a blast with your husband?

2. *Show You* Care.

This one is a biggie. As women, we like when our husband does thoughtful things just to let us know he's thinking of us; we need to do the same for him.

There are big ways and countless small ways we can show our spouse we care. Fold a load of his laundry that he hasn't had time to finish. Sneak a Hallmark card into his briefcase. Plan a date that centers around all of his favorite things. Give him the last piece of gum in your pack when everything in you wants to keep it for yourself.

I bet you can think of some creative, inexpensive ways to show your husband you care. Don't wait on him to do special things for you first. Go ahead and set the precedent. Why not make it a goal to do a least one random act of kindness for your spouse every week?

Also keep in mind, as we discussed in a previous chapter, men long to feel *respected* by their wives. That said, we'll undermine our acts of kindness if our words and attitudes often convey disrespect. One of the major ways we show we care is by affirming just how much we value our husband as a provider, father, lover, and best friend.

Just like a little salt can make a good meal even better, a couple that seasons their marriage with thoughtful, caring words and gestures will have a much more satisfying relationship.

3. *Expect* Change.

The only thing that never changes is that life is always changing. While I am fairly confident you will not have to deal with Edward and Bella's first marital difficulty—getting pregnant with a half-human, half-vampire life-sucking fetus—you and your mate are most certainly going to go through some life changes and challenges as individuals and also as a couple. Financial fluctuations, job losses and transfers, new life aspirations, and unexpected trying circumstances all likely lie ahead in your future. However, we must determine to grow *together* with our spouse during these unfamiliar times, as opposed to allowing change to pull us apart.

The key to staying united as a couple throughout all of life's changing seasons is to stay united to Christ.

4. *Follow* Christ.

My husband and I like to use the images on the following page to illustrate the opposing ways a couple can approach marriage. The man and woman who keep Christ at the center of their relationship continually draw closer to God and to each other, as portrayed in the top image. The man and woman who do *not* serve Christ but instead focus on their own individual self-centered agendas find themselves in a never-ending, futile tug-o-war. It's exhausting, they grow further and further apart, and nobody wins. They fight to get what they want, dragging their mate through the proverbial mud if that's what it takes to get their way.

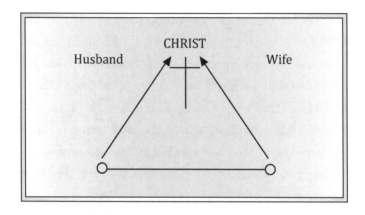

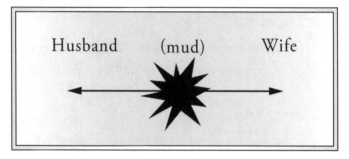

A pastor once shared the following story, and it sheds light on the two images above. A couple came to him for marital counseling. The disgruntled woman went on and on about how awful her husband was, then he defended himself against her accusations by reciting all of her shortcomings. This miserable verbal tennis match carried on for half an hour. When the couple finally quit hurling insults at each other and looked at the pastor, hoping he would declare which one of them was right, he shocked them with the following statement: "I've got great news for you two! You don't have a marital problem at all!"

Looking bewildered, they asked for clarification. The pastor explained, "You don't have a marital problem, *you're just the lousiest Christians I've ever met.*" He then got up and walked out, leaving the couple alone to contemplate the seriousness of his words. A short time later, the couple exited his office hand in hand and thanked the pastor for his candid reality check.

I've said it over and over throughout this book—Christ is the difference maker in a relationship. When a couple makes the effort to learn about Him together, serve and obey Him together, and pray to God together, they tend to *stay happy* together.

5. *Get* Counsel.

Don't let the counseling story I just shared with you scare you! One of the most beneficial actions a couple can take when struggling with conflict is to seek out wise counsel. Bear in mind that not everyone with a state counselor's license is wise. Who you go to for counseling is vitally important. Having said that, every couple needs someone who will offer godly counsel, unbiased insight, and practical solutions to marital discord. I hate to think how many divorced couples could have overcome their marital obstacles if only they had taken their issues to a qualified, Christ-filled counselor.

Don't be too proud to get help. We all need a third-party's perspective and advice at some point. And going to a counselor doesn't mean we're crazy; it means we're sick of certain issues *driving us crazy*, and we're ready for solutions.

6. *Keep Your* Commitment.

Why is it that we vow to stand by our mate "for better or for worse," then when things get worse, we think we have the right to bail out of the marriage? Do we really believe we'll be happier with someone else? A new man simply means new issues; that's all.

Keeping our marital commitment does *not* mean we stay in a miserable marriage. On the contrary, it means that we refuse to settle for a miserable marriage. We determine to invest our prayers, time, energy, and creativity into improving our relationship with our husband.

Unfortunately, one person's willingness to work on the marriage cannot entirely compensate for an unwilling spouse. In such cases, we have to rely on God's grace to move on our husband's heart and show us what to do, one day at a time.

DON'T JUST SURVIVE—THRIVE!

Edward and Bella aren't just moderately fond of each other, and they don't merely put up with each other—they are madly in love! That should always be our goal as well.

Don't sweep conflict under the rug or settle for a loveless marriage. Agreeing to stay married until the kids graduate is *not* acceptable. You can't fool children. They may not realize how bad things have truly gotten between you and your spouse, but they are well aware when Mom and Dad lack genuine affection and companionship. If you want to do right by your kids, let them see you and your husband love each other with sincerity, unwavering commitment, and passion.

Isn't that what we love about Edward and Bella?

REFLECTIONS ON ROMANCE—CHAPTER 9

1. Explain in your own words why newlyweds go from utter bliss to relational challenges. Do you feel prepared to persevere when times get tough? Why or why not?

_____

_____

_____

_____

2. (Single readers) Do you know a married couple who seem to be disconnected in their relationship? How does seeing their relationship make you feel?

(Married readers) Have you become disconnected from your spouse? If so, how did it happen, and what can you do about it?

_____

_____

_____

_____

_____

3. What happens to a couple when both he and she focus on their self-centered agendas and do not serve Christ?

_____

_____

_____

_____

4. Do you believe it's vitally important to keep your marital commitment? Why?

_____

_____

_____

_____

5. Write down a promise to yourself—that you will not settle for lifeless love, but that you will do whatever it takes to make sure your marriage thrives throughout the years.

_____

_____

_____

_____

PRAYER

God, we know from Your Word that the marriage covenant is near and dear to Your heart. We also know You intend that our marriage do more than merely exist; You want our love to thrive. Father, I pray that my relationship with my spouse would continually improve over the years, and that we will always invest in the time, energy, prayers, and patience it takes to experience a satisfying marriage. Help us to keep Christ at the center of our focus, both individually and as a couple.

Endnote

1. Stephenie Meyer, *Breaking Dawn* (New York: Hachette Book Group USA, 2008), 49.

Chapter Ten

SATISFIED

 Am I ready to meet my "Edward" now?

*I'm thinking that you have made it all the way to the last chapter of this book because you have a deep desire to experience a **real** love story of your own. You want real passion and attraction, real romance and laughter, and real commitment that not only stands the test of time, but has a way of seemingly making time stand still.*

If I thought, for one minute, God was unable to bring your love-related desires to pass, I never would have written this book. But that's just it; I *do* believe He is able to do exceedingly abundantly above all you could ever ask or think (see Eph. 3:20).

The question is, *are you ready?* Are you prepared to begin a relationship with "Edward"? Are you willing to love him—for better or worse—till death do you part?

Here are a few personal reflection questions to consider along those lines:

ARE YOU OK WITH YOU?

As we've previously discussed, having a guy in your life—even a fantastic guy—is not the secret to happiness, nor is it the cure for feeling poorly about yourself. If you're insecure now, you'll be insecure with "Edward." If you're depressed now, you'll eventually be depressed with "Edward." If you feel wounded in your soul now, you'll feel wounded with "Edward." I'm sure you're starting to see the pattern.

There's a difference in having an intense longing to be with your soul mate (or a strong desire for a deeper connection with your spouse) and believing you can't live life without "Edward." Furthermore, until you are OK standing on your own two feet and relying on God's grace to give you the strength to embrace each day with joy, you aren't ready to build a life with "Edward."

None of us is ready to love a man until we first understand how much God loves us, and therefore, love and accept ourselves.

HAVE YOU FORGIVEN THE MEN IN YOUR LIFE?

If at some point in your distant or not-so-distant past, a man did something that hurt or seriously disappointed you, you must come to a place where you can forgive and release any ongoing resentment or bitterness. Although you will likely never forget the wrong done to you, your willingness to let go and let God bring ultimate judgment concerning that situation will enable you to love "Edward" with your whole heart. On the contrary, holding onto a grudge toward a man, whether it be our father, a relative, or a former "sweetie," can cause us to project those same negative feelings onto "Edward." This can result in an unwarranted distrust or resentment toward him, which can destroy what would have been a satisfying relationship.

HAVE YOU CUT OFF COMMUNICATION WITH "JACOB"?

As previously discussed in Chapter 7, we need to free ourselves from any lingering dead-end relationships with guys who we know are not "the one." This means we end communication and move on, as opposed to keeping in contact based on the notion that we are "just friends" now. Even if nothing more than friendly contact has occurred for a while, we owe it to both "Jacob" and "Edward"—not to mention, ourselves—to snuff out the burning embers with old flames completely.

DOES LIFE HAVE TO REVOLVE AROUND YOU?

Self-centeredness comes natural to all of us, and it requires effort, God's grace, and spiritual maturity in order to overcome me-obsessed living. That said, your relationship with "Edward" won't end in *happily ever after* if you are a self-absorbed person. Those who insist on getting their way all of the time and can't stomach making personal sacrifices for someone else's benefit are not ready to love "Edward." Love, by its very nature, requires that we humble ourselves and invest in another's happiness, even if it means forgoing our own gratification at times.

When we realize that life is *not* all about our personal agenda and wants, we are far better prepared to build a life with "Edward."

Are you willing to wait?

If you feel you just *have* to meet "Edward" right this minute or you just might turn blue and suffocate, you're not likely to meet him at all. (Along those same lines, if you are impatient with your spouse and want him to make drastic changes overnight, he will sense your intolerance and resent you for it.)

In the quest to find the right fish in the sea, a heart that bleeds with impatience tends to attract blood-thirsty sharks—guys looking to take advantage of a female's romantic desperation.

Can I give you two "do nots"?

Do not cling to the wrong guy out of impatience.

Do not pressure someone to marry you.

You don't want to be with some obsessive, stalker-like guy who insists on getting married before you feel ready, do you? Well "Edward" doesn't want to be with a woman like that, either. So don't be like that! Be patient and give love time to develop.

Obviously, if you're an adult and have been seeing a guy for years, but he has some fear-of-commit-ment-and-marriage-thing going on, that's a different story. In that case, I don't advise staying with him for a decade waiting on a marriage proposal. That said, I must lovingly point out that a woman who is not willing to have premarital sex almost never finds herself in that predicament.

OK, I'M READY FOR MY MAN!

Perhaps you passed the "Are You Ready Test" with flying colors, and now your expectancy and hope of loving for a lifetime are at an all-time high. Great! One of the main goals I had in writing this book was to encourage you that romance *is* still alive and that we have *every right* to desire and seek out passionate, lasting love.

Having said that, I don't want to leave you intoxicated by the sweet aroma of the roses without being honest with you about the thorns.

Hopefully after reading the previous chapters you understand that all relationships require work and sacrifice, and every couple struggles at times. Loving for life requires that we resist all kinds of temptations and selfish tendencies, but the benefits of keeping our family intact and our soul mate in our arms is worth it. Most of us will grow old and look back at what turned out to be a long, satisfying journey with our spouse. But what about those whose dreams of life with "Edward" get shattered by unforeseen circumstances?

Allow me to introduce you to my dear friend Brody.

BRODY'S STORY

I met Brody when I was a young teenager and he was in college. As a friend of the family, he came over now and then, and he and I had a blast trying to beat the "Grand Puma" in a Nintendo boxing videogame. Brody was very good looking, highly intelligent, and he loved the Lord.

He graduated from the prestigious United States Naval Academy, where he was an all-American in boxing and fencing and later inducted into the Naval Academy Athletic Hall of Fame. Brody became a pilot and lieutenant commander, eventually earning a bronze star and air medal for his valiant actions over Afghanistan.

This guy was destined to be one lucky lady's "Edward." Soon, Brody met that lucky young woman, and they fell in love and became husband and wife. The happy couple was elated when their baby girl came along, and they welcomed yet another little one into the world a few years later, a boy this time.

All was well with their family when Brody began experiencing an odd physical challenge. He realized he was increasingly slurring his speech. Puzzled, he went to the doctor and had a series of tests run. He and his wife were shocked and devastated by the diagnosis. Brody had Lou Gehrig's disease, a fatal disorder that steadily destroys the neuromuscular system, causing one to rapidly lose motor function until the body finally succumbs to death. The news came at a horrible time; his wife was pregnant with their third baby.

At just 31 years of age, Brody struggled to comprehend the reality of his situation. With his wife by his side, he resolved to fight the disease, symbolized by his participation in a marathon he ran just days after his grim diagnosis. As determined as Brody and his wife were, however, Brody's condition worsened. Three years later, he could not speak and had little ability to move.

By this time, news of Brody's physical battle reached my family, and we began praying. One night in particular, I couldn't sleep and felt a sense of urgency to intercede in prayer for him and his family. I went into the living room and took advantage of the quiet stillness that hovered over my household in the middle of the night. Not sure exactly what to pray, I asked God to surround Brody, his wife, and their kids with His loving presence. I prayed for their comfort and strength during this treacherous time in their lives.

The next morning, I received a phone call and the heart-sinking news that Brody had passed away in the middle of the night. I suddenly understood why the Lord woke me to pray. I thought of Brody's children, his parents, his brothers and sisters, and I cried. My heart was especially heavy, however, for his wife. On December 5, 2005, she buried the father of her young children, her handsome lover. They planned to live a long, adventurous life together and grow old side by side, but on this day, she reluctantly whispered goodbye to her heart's hero.

As her husband's body was lowered into the ground, her love-related dreams were buried with him.

THE GOOD NEWS

Believe it or not, I shared Brody's story with you, not to depress or discourage you, but actually to encourage you with some good news. You see, even when life takes a drastic turn for the worst and dearly held plans end in shocking disappointment, there is hope. *How*, you ask? Because there is one even more faithful, loving, courageous, committed, powerful, and loyal than "Edward," and this supernatural man will *never* leave us. I'm talking about *Jesus Christ*.

You may hear that name and feel a rush of comfort and reassurance. Then again, you may envision some old painting hanging in your grandmother's dining room where Jesus is pictured wearing a formal robe with a stoic expression and an odd glowing headband-type object floating above His head. Make no mistake about it though; Jesus is much more than a mere historical figure, more than some man in a painting. He's the hero in the world's greatest love story, the champion that literally saved the human race! What's more, He's the ultimate answer to our soul's need to feel loved, protected, and valued, and He wants a personal, meaningful relationship *with you*. If you're unsure how to begin a relationship with Christ, I've included some helpful information in the Appendix, a summary entitled, "So You've Got Faith-Related Doubts?" and a quiz for self-reflection entitled, "Am I a Good Person?"

When we give Christ preeminence in our heart and look to God as our ultimate source of peace, contentment, and love, we don't have to fear what the future holds because we know that whatever life brings, Jesus will walk through it with us. He laughs with us on the mountain tops, perseveres with us through desert lands, and embraces and grieves with us in the depths of life's valleys. No matter what happens, we are never alone. He's there to guide, comfort, and sustain us. That's good news for you and for me! That's the kind of news that gives a young widow the strength to face each day with hope.

I once saw a bumper sticker that said, "Is God your steering wheel or your spare tire?" The implication, of course, is that we can either surrender our lives to God daily in loving worship and obedience or put Him out of our heart and mind until we get in a bind of some sort and need a miracle. Friend, determine to love God with all of the commitment and passion you have. Love Him with your every breath, until your last breath. Love Him as the ultimate "Edward" in your life, the one-and-only who gave His life for you.

Love Him because He first loved you, and because—should your world come crashing down around you—His love will cover you.

A BLESSING FROM MY HEART TO YOURS

Thank you for taking this journey with me and reading the words that the Lord placed on my heart for you. As you courageously seek to love and be loved, may you sense God's presence, follow His leading, and experience the miracle of romantic passion and heartfelt commitment. I pray that your beauty and nurturing spirit captivates the heart of a handsome, God-fearing man. May you always feel valued, appreciated, and treasured by the one to whom you choose to give your heart. And may you seize every opportunity to honor and respect your spouse, esteeming him with such adoration that he becomes endeared to you always.

I ask the Lord to protect you from evil temptations that would destroy your family. I pray that you delight in your husband and children throughout life's many seasons, and find great joy caring for your household. May your children's children behold the lasting love that exudes from your marriage as an example they can follow.

May you revel in God's love and continually rejoice in the love that you have for your one-and-only.

REFLECTIONS ON ROMANCE—CHAPTER 10

Having read the book in its entirety, summarize the lingering thoughts and life lessons that have now become a part of who you are, along with how you will choose to love God and your mate from this day on.

_____

_____

_____

_____

_____

_____

_____

_____

_____

_____

_____

_____

_____

_____

_____

Endnote

1. Stephenie Meyer, *Breaking Dawn* (New York: Hachette Book Group USA, 2008), 741.

Appendix

SO YOU'VE GOT FAITH-RELATED DOUBTS?

You may have crossed paths with a Christian at some point who got irritated—perhaps even downright angry with you—because you expressed some faith-related doubts. Well, that's not the reaction you're going to get from me, my friend. After all, I've viewed life through the lens of a spiritual skeptic myself. That said, I'm a firm believer that until we wrestle with a certain amount of doubt, it's not possible to experience lasting faith. Furthermore, faith is not the total absence of doubt, but rather, a trust based on reasonable evidence that makes it possible to sincerely believe.

That said, if you question the existence of God, aren't convinced the Bible is a supernatural book, consider all religions equally valid (even though they teach contrary things), and question whether Jesus Christ was a mere mortal man or God in human form, please do me a favor. Do your due diligence to look objectively into these matters.

I've met one person in my lifetime who called himself an atheist but had a strong desire to discover evidence in favor of God's existence. All the other atheistic friends I've had over the years were reluctant to hear *anything* that might shatter their theories of a Godless universe. I said that to say that, whatever your stance is as it pertains to faith and religion, be open to discovery. More than that; pursue the truth with your whole heart and mind. That's what I did, and I'm so glad I persevered! While I'm still seeking answers to some questions, I was able to settle the core faith-related issues which I formerly approached with skepticism and doubt.

Arriving at logical, reasonable conclusions about spirituality and religion transformed my life dramatically and permanently. (If I'm being honest, the source of my transformation was not so much *what* I learned but *who* the evidence and discoveries led me to—I'm referring to my Savior, Jesus Christ.)

I urge you to take the following quiz, "Am I a good person?" If you find yourself questioning some of the statements I make, I dare you to try and disprove me. I don't say that in arrogance, but rather, with a sincere desire to see you seek out spiritual truth for yourself. Along those lines, here are a few excellent resources I recommend:

- Concerning God's existence and Creationism, *www.AnswersInGenesis.org.*
- Concerning the Bible and Jesus Christ, *www.LeeStrobal.com.*
- Concerning world religions and a Biblical worldview, *www.TheTruthProject.org.*
Faith and Doubt, by John Ortberg.

QUIZ

"Would Edward Choose You?"

1. Do you think you're a good person?
   ☐ Yes ☐ No

Let me guess, you checked *yes*. After all, you've never killed anyone and you try to do good things when you have the opportunity, right? I'm sure compared to the average "Joe" you truly are an outstanding citizen.

2. Are you familiar with the Ten Commandments?
   ☐ Yes ☐ No

While we tend to compare ourselves to other people, like criminals for example, in order to feel good about the kind of person we are, God gave us the Ten Commandments as the standard or "measuring stick" we could use to evaluate our personal goodness. (See Exodus 20.) Let's look at three of the commandments and see how we measure up.

3. Have you ever lied?
   ☐ Yes   ☐ No

Of course you have—we have all broken this commandment. As a matter of fact, if you said no, you're lying! And what do we call people who lie? Yep, we call them *liars* (or no-good rotten stinkin' liars if it's someone who lied to us personally).

4. Have you/Did you ever disobey your parents?
   ☐ Yes   ☐ No

If I was a gambling gal, I'd bet the farm that you have deliberately disobeyed your parents on more than one occasion (I don't own a farm, but you get the point). I wasn't exactly a perfect angel growing up myself, so I am just as guilty of breaking this commandment as you are. Friend, you and I have been *rebellious,* haven't we?

5. Have you ever stolen anything?

☐ Yes ☐ No

OK, maybe you haven't robbed a bank at gunpoint, but have you ever taken something that didn't belong to you? I remember taking money out of a girl's purse in the locker room in junior high. Pathetic, I know. And what do we call people who steal? Not stealers—*thieves.*

6. Do you still think you're a good person?

☐ Yes ☐ No

We've looked at just three of the Ten Commandments and already you and I have proven to be lying, thieving, rebellious people! To make matters worse, the Bible says God is going to judge us by those Ten Commandments. So what's the verdict on you?

7. Do you think you would be found innocent or guilty?

☐ Umm...innocent ☐ Guilty

If you said innocent, I just have one thing to say— "Denial, party of one, your table is now available!" You have broken God's Laws just like I have, and we are guilty. To deny that we are guilty of breaking God's Law is illogical. Our own conscience bears witness of our guilt every time we do something wrong, doesn't it?

8. What do you plan to do about your guilt?

☐ Try to make up for it by doing good things, like going to church and giving money to the poor.

☐ Hope I discover a fountain of immortality so I never have to die and stand before God to give account for my actions.

☐ Nothing; there's nothing I can do about it.

If you said you plan to do good things to make up for your guilt, I have some bad news for you—God will not accept that. Think about it, would a good judge let a man guilty of murder go free because he had volunteered at a food pantry a few times? I know you've never murdered anyone, but Jesus said if we've ever hated anyone, we have committed murder in our hearts (ouch!) (see Matt. 5:21-22). The truth is there's really nothing we can do to erase our guilt. If we try to quit sinning, we will only get frustrated because we can't completely stop; besides, it wouldn't change the fact that we have sinned in the past.

9. What do you think will happen if you stand before God guilty of breaking the Ten Commandments?

☐ He'll understand I meant well and let me into Heaven anyway.

☐ I'll go to hell.

If Heaven is a perfect place like the Bible describes, yet God is willing to simply wink at our sin and let liars, thieves, and rebellious people like us in, Heaven wouldn't be perfect for long, would it? The Bible is clear that all sinners are separated from God relationally and, therefore, upon dying, go to the place where His presence cannot be found—hell.

10. Does that concern you?

☐ Not really ☐ YES!

Right now while you're young and healthy, it may be easy to say that you're not worried about where you will go when you die, but what do you think it would be like to be on your death bed, knowing you are going to face eternity and God any minute? Of course, it's a terrifying thought to think that we could end up in hell, separated from God forever...and ever...and ever...and ever...OK, my brain hurts!

11. Is God a big fat "meanie"?

☐ It kind of seems that way!   ☐ No

If God knew good and darn well that you and I couldn't keep the Ten Commandments and we would just end up in hell, why did He give us those blasted commandments in the first place? Allow me to answer that important question. God gave us the Ten Commandments so we would realize we can't keep them, thus, we would recognize our need for a Savior (i.e., Jesus Christ). You see, man is intrinsically proud and self-reliant, but God's Commandments act as a mirror and show us how "ugly" we really are. It's only when we see our true reflection in the mirror of God's Laws that we come to understand reality, which is that we are desperate for God's intervention and help!

12. Do you know what God did so that you don't have to be punished for your sins?

☐ He told mankind we could all just make up what we think is the way to Heaven and He would honor all of our creative ideas.

☐ He sent His Son, Jesus Christ, to take the punishment we deserve.

While there are a variety of religions to choose from, only *one* actually deals with the issue at hand—man's broken relationship with God as a result of our sin. Every world religion involves earning one's right standing (righteousness) with God through good works, except one; *Christianity*. Romans 6:23 says, *"For the wages* [earned consequences] *of sin is death* [physical and eternal separation from God], *but the free gift of God is eternal life through Christ Jesus..."* (NLT). In other words, the punishment and payment for our sins was impossible for any of us to pay, so God lovingly paid it for us by sending His Son, Jesus Christ, to be punished in our place (by death on the cross). Simply put, humanity has one huge problem—sin—and God gave one mandatory solution—Jesus Christ. It really is that simple.

13. So how do I go about getting forgiven?

☐ Just say some little prayer about inviting Jesus into your heart and then you never have to think about all that spiritual stuff anymore; you're safe from hell.

☐ Read your Bible all day everyday and never sin again and then Jesus will accept you.

☐ Repent for your sins and start a new life with Jesus as your Lord and Savior.

We don't get saved by repeating some prayer that we don't really mean and then living the same old self-centered life we always have. We also don't get saved by being "good religious folk" who memorize the Bible and try to be perfect. Salvation is relational, meaning it occurs not by *what we do*, but by *who we choose* to love and trust. We simply:

- *Acknowledge our sin* instead of making excuses and trying to justify our actions (see 1 John 1:9).

- *Repent for our sinful heart,* which means we turn away from a life of self-centeredness and self-reliance apart from God and rely on Him instead (see Acts 2:37-39).

- *Accept Christ's sacrifice on our behalf* by acknowledging that we cannot earn salvation but must receive it based on what Christ already did for us on the cross (see Rom. 6:23).

- *Commit to live for Christ* out of a heart of gratitude for the fact that He died for us (see Gal. 2:20).

14. Is there a formal prayer I need to pray?
    ☐ Yes, you must pray certain words while seated in a certain position in a

certain place on a certain day of the
week for a certain amount of time.

☐ Nope!

Just pray from your heart. The Bible says when you confess and turn from your sins and put your trust in Christ, the Holy Spirit will literally come and dwell in you and lead you for the rest of your life to the degree that you yield to His leadership (see Eph. 1:13-14). Cool, huh?

15. Does this mean I'll never sin again?

☐ Yep, and you can walk on water, too!

☐ No, we're not 100% sin-free until we die and shed our "fallen" nature.

While we will never totally triumph over sin in this life, we can have lots of victories along the way if we rely on the Holy Spirit to help us resist and overcome temptation.

In conclusion, committing sins is a big deal because sin is what separates us from God. Even after we repent for our sins and pursue a relationship with Christ, we are still tempted to sin. Yes, the blood of Jesus covers our sins when we mess up, but we don't like sinning because the Holy Spirit lives in us and He gives us new desires. We *want* to do what's right. Furthermore, when we love God, we desire to please

Him and follow His ways because we are grateful for His presence in our lives.

So what do you think? Do you need to have a little "heart-to-heart" with God? I tell you what, having that talk with God was the best thing I ever did—not because life has been easy since then, but because I now know what I'm living for.

LAURA GALLIER

is on a mission to:

- *Equip parents to inspire sexual purity in their kids,
- *Empower teens and singles to make solid decisions concerning sex and their future, and
- *Encourage people of all ages with a Biblical understanding of sex and purity-related standards.

Laura partners with parents, churches, and organizations to avail her materials, workshops, presentations, and ongoing support.

www.lauragallier.com

In the right hands, This Book will Change Lives!

Most of the people who need this message will not be looking for this book. To change their lives, you need to put a copy of this book in their hands.

> *But others (seeds) fell into good ground, and brought forth fruit, some a hundred-fold, some sixty-fold, some thirty-fold* (Matthew 13:8).

Our ministry is constantly seeking methods to find the good ground, the people who need this anointed message to change their lives. Will you help us reach these people?

> *Remember this—a farmer who plants only a few seeds will get a small crop. But the one who plants generously will get a generous crop* (2 Corinthians 9:6).

EXTEND THIS MINISTRY BY SOWING
3 BOOKS, 5 BOOKS, 10 BOOKS, OR MORE TODAY,
AND BECOME A LIFE CHANGER!

Thank you,

Don Nori Sr., Publisher
Destiny Image
Since 1982

DESTINY IMAGE PUBLISHERS, INC.

"Speaking to the Purposes of God for This Generation and for the Generations to Come."

VISIT OUR NEW SITE HOME AT
WWW.DESTINYIMAGE.COM

FREE SUBSCRIPTION TO DI NEWSLETTER

Receive free unpublished articles by top DI authors, exclusive discounts, and free downloads from our best and newest books.

Visit www.destinyimage.com to subscribe.

Write to: Destiny Image
               P.O. Box 310
               Shippensburg, PA 17257-0310

Call: 1-800-722-6774

Email: orders@destinyimage.com

For a complete list of our titles or to place an order online, visit www.destinyimage.com.